# THE SEASONAL EYE

# THE SEASONAL EYE

Keith Taylor

The Book Guild Ltd

First published in Great Britain in 2023 by
The Book Guild Ltd
Unit E2 Airfield Business Park,
Harrison Road, Market Harborough,
Leicestershire. LE16 7UL
Tel: 0116 2792299
www.bookguild.co.uk
Email: info@bookguild.co.uk
Twitter: @bookguild



Typeset in 11pt Minion Pro

Printed and bound in Great Britain by 4edge Limited

ISBN 9781915603975

British Library Cataloguing in Publication Data.
A catalogue record for this book is available from the British Library.

# OTHER PUBLICATIONS BY KEITH TAYLOR

## CHILDREN'S NATURAL HISTORY

*Foxes* A & C Black

## REGIONAL

*Nostalgic Look at Wollaton* Robin Hood Publishing
*Wollaton Remembered* Tempus Publishing
*Trent Lock and the Erewash Canal* The History Press
*Old Nottinghamshire Remembered* Sigma Press
*Exploring Nottingham* Amberley

## WALKING

*Rambles Around Nottingham and Derby* Sigma Press
*Favourite Walks in Three Counties* Five Leaves Publishing

## OCCULT/PHENOMENA

*Ghosts of Wollaton* Halls of Derby
*Beyond the Midnight Chill* Long Skein Publishing

## POETRY

*Ancestor Connection* Long Skein Publishing
*Gold Fever* Long Skein Publishing
*Background Detail* Long Skein Publishing
*Sunset Windows* Long Skein Publishing
*After the Snowfall* Long Skein Publishing

## AUTOBIOGRAPHY

*The Uncertainties of Morning* Manuscript Publishing

## FICTION (Humour)

*Something of a National Treasure* eBook Amazon

## SHORT STORIES

*In the Heat Haze* Long Skein Publishing

## NATURAL HISTORY

*Getting to Know Our Everyday Birds* Long Skein Publishing

What is this life if, full of care,
we have no time to stand and stare?

W H Davies

# JANUARY

## Hobhole Drain, Lincolnshire

The dampness aside, if the winter nurtures a smell it is that of cold metal. Aloof, unfriendly, daring us to step over its weather-threatening barriers.

Snow slants across the windscreen as we negotiate the winding lanes between Sedgebrook and Grimsthorpe on the east Leicestershire-west Lincolnshire border. On the inner side of the hedgerow, being concertinaed by the fury of the blizzard wind, a black fallow deer doe stands cropping ivy leaves and possibly the offerings of small plum-like berry crop also.

This strain of fallow deer is said to have been introduced to Britain from the forests of Norway by the hunting-conscious King James I. The more commonly seen 'menil' strain, with fawn or russet coat pebble-dashed with white, were in all probability introduced by the Romans who, it is thought, kept them on their ships during their voyages as sources of food. Be that as it may, fallow deer are not indigenous to Britain, a fact near proven by the awareness that, in contrast to our native red deer, fallow need to take in very little water. They seem to suffice on the moisture they take from our grasslands. *They drink*, of that there can be no doubt, but seldom, if ever, bathe. Thus the zoologist becomes aware of a species that – like many types of antelope – belongs to the hot plains of the eastern countries and, due to that, have adapted to a relatively dry, although sometimes shaded, environment here in Britain.

Fallow deer are now recorded as roaming wild in every English county and have been for the past two or three decades. They have their well-established paths extending across country from fields to coverts and on to both deciduous tracts of woodland and the pine forested acres largely established by the Forestry Commission.

Way on along the route taking us to the Witham Estuary, I reflect that this morning's black doe had journeyed purposely across her range of chosen acres to feed on the stand of roadside ivy as she and possibly others do throughout these bleak and sometimes featureless winter months.

The eye of a deer at 20 feet is barely discernible, whereas the eye we are seeking today, while not large, is well rounded and if seen in or around haw or blackthorn thickets in sunlight aided by a birdwatcher's 'scope is an arresting jewel in every sense of the word. Surrounding the expected black pupil is a circle of deep orange that may appear reddish in certain streams of light.

On the journey out to this relatively coastal edgeland we may have passed several thickets and woods – serving as winter roosting quarters for long-eared owls – but here, according to my son Stuart, several long-eared owls are relatively easy to pick out, deep and roosting among the haw and blackthorn thickets as they are.

Hobhole Drain in the winter takes the surplus water from the fields out and around East Flow and Friskney to the mouth of the River Witham where it joins The Wash near the market town of Boston.

On a January morning of plunging temperatures I can recommend it to few other than those who are lured out by the prospect of glimpsing one or more of these splendid and elusive birds.

Although the basic image is that of a bird, which frequents and breeds in tracts of pine forest, the long-eared owl is, during the winter, often located in daylight roosting in high and relatively isolated thickets.

As quite a number of ornithologists are aware, the thickets bordering Hobhole Drain have attracted long-eared owls for quite some years now. They could be the European forest strain that breed in Finland and Scandinavia and make the sea crossing well ahead of the northern winter.

The ear tufts of the long-eared owl are raised when the bird is listening for sounds of prey or potential mobsters like the blackbird and magpie homing in, but are occasionally lowered and held relatively close to the head during periods of digestive rest and roosting.

On prospecting this area a few days ago Stuart, to his delight, encountered two long-eared owls sunning themselves in full view of anyone walking the strip road on the opposite side of the drain. It was from this road that he viewed them through binoculars and compared their plumage differences, one being a 'grey phased' long-eared owl, the other a warm brown or 'rufous' phase.

Blackbird called 'picka-pik' as they arrowed by the berry harvests. More than one paused to display aggression and attempt to mob one or both owls, which remained statuesque and, like the thickets, reflected in the mud-coloured water surface below.

Today breath mists before us and our eyes water within seconds of having stepped from the vehicle. There is not a long-eared owl in sight. The freezing east wind and these gusts of sleety rain have persuaded them to seek roosts deeper within the thickets. Nevertheless, on scanning the mass of haw branches through binoculars, a rufous patch flares against the greenish yellows of last autumn's dismembered foliage.

The owl is perched in profile but with long-eared tufts discernible. The blotches and streaks on its plumage blend well with its surroundings.

When a cock blackbird attempts to perch in front of the owl to pluck a haw berry from a cluster, the owl turns its head to reveal – yes – the distinctive orange buff facial disc and those reddish-orange eyes highlighting the staring black pupils within. Eureka! My trophy taken and not a bullet spent in having to do it.

While scanning the thickets for other owls I recalled a summer evening in the 'way back' hearing the calls of a pair which, although unseen, were feeding and attracting young out of the nest – previously a grey squirrel drey – high in a pine situated in the heart of the Clipstone and

Rufford Forest in Nottinghamshire. With a companion I was screened by ground foliage and watching a fox cub exploring the roots, bark and branches of a gale-felled silver birch. In the background a magpie rattled, then the sudden 'hooo-oo' of a protesting and equally agitated long-eared owl was cause enough for the owlets to give out their reedy calls thus indicating that they were waiting for the adult pair to fly in with prey.

We heard most of the long-eared owl's varied vocabulary on that sultry evening. Weeks later, Matt, a work colleague, described being out in a clear felled area of the forest at dusk with the intention of watching nightjars when a large rufous owl swept from a pine branch and over the clear area. Due to its immediate lack of ear tufts, to the human eye at least, Matt identified it as a tawny owl, a species which, inland, shares the same habitat. But then ear tufts appeared when the predator located a small bird or rodent in the vegetation below and silently swept over the area to claim its prey in the manner of a harrier. And so Matt later recorded in his notebook his first sighting of a long-eared owl.

Leaving the Hobhole Drain hedgers and ditchers path, satisfied with that glimpse of the very bird species we were hoping to locate, Stuart and I take the grassed footpath which follows a hedgeline across the side of arable land.

The ditch, as ever overhung by hawthorn thickets, holds stands of reed and sedge. Out to our right, the direction from which the cheek-smarting wind continues slapping our faces, the grey-brown mudflats and creeks of the strand line known as Boston Deeps attempt to thwart the faintest suggestion of a coastal horizon. We flush blackbirds, and occasional wren and meadow pipit, from the hedgerow. But the brown rat, perched squirrel-like in a hawthorn cleft as it plucks and nibbles berries, refuses to leave despite our proximity.

We walk, hearing only the prolonged whine of the wind, until the musical trills of a redshank and yodelling of an oystercatcher sharpens my senses.

Glassing a group of diving duck in an arm of seawater I pass over a scaup drake, taking it for a tufted drake. And not for the first time in Stuart's tutorial presence.

## Wildfowl Trust, Slimbridge, Gloucestershire

A winter sunset and a V formation created by a family of mute swans, full winged and flying in to feed with the whooper and Bewick swans congregating to devour the grain scattered over the surface of Rushy Pen.

The cob of this mute swan family carries already the black knob or 'berry' at the base of his bill, a sign that the breeding season, although weeks away yet, will see him and his mate rearing another brood of cygnets after having dispersed the four flying with them this late afternoon.

As always I pause to watch the mute swans bank against the background flares of the sunset which momentarily swathes them in pink as, with 7-feet wingspans still creating the winter sky music, each drops black paddles from its underparts to make the spectacular landing. Like all birds and mammals, the swans are intent on gaining a last food intake before the freezing cloak of night settles in.

Out beyond the reserve and along country roadsides the length and breadth of Britain, people – *motorists mainly* – will glimpse a kestrel hovering; a sparrowhawk darting into a finch-tenanted hedgerow; carrion crows; jackdaws and magpies inspecting the verges for roadkill victims; flocks of titmice seeking both a roost and an intake of bird food, fat or suet. Almost every entity is, in its own way, hunting. Needing to take in food, a store of energy, to see it through the cruel, black hours ahead.

Just offset from the Slimbridge observatory a bird feeder is positioned so as to allow the small birds in but keep the pestering grey squirrels – should there be any – out.

Tawny streak bound running to a direct point beneath the feeder – *weasel.* If it has seen us its quest for food supersedes its natural caution. It may well be a local regular, like the incoming family of mute swans.

The weasel pauses, sniffs the ground. Muddy, soured and with peanuts ground in by a warden's boots as he or she attended to the bird feeder earlier.

With our seasonal eyes connecting to the brain we recognise but one entity – the weasel. But there could well be two. Unseen by ourselves and the weasel in which the nematode parasite may be thriving. The veterinary officer, who twice showed me the skulls of stoats and weasels which had inadvertently hosted nematodes, was awed by the neatness of the holes in the skulls while further explaining that the poor creatures had undoubtedly suffered fits before succumbing to the inevitable.

To a layman naturalist like myself, it is enough to learn that the nematodes are taken in when the stoats or weasel kill and eat mice. The nematodes, or red roundworms, take refuge in the host's nostrils, travel into the sinuses, eating and feeding along through to the spine. Here they are believed to breed, male to female nematode parasite, and lay their eggs. Thus the body of the hosting stoat or weasel becomes swiftly riddled with nematodes in their differing stages of growth and breeding development.

Obviously the monitoring of nematodes is a microscopic study concluding in the publications of scientific papers.

However, I would like to think that the weasel waiting for a dunnock or robin to settle on the ground beneath the bird feeder may be free of hosting parasites. But in this particular case what the seasonal eye cannot see may, on the other hand, eventually drive the little hunter into a mammalian form of insanity.

## Breaston, South Derbyshire

Attracted to the wood-burning stove, the solitary pivotal point of comfort on this raw morning, I asked the farm shop manager if lambing is in progress in the sheds at the rear of the farm shop and garden centre.

Placing and positioning an ash log in the seething red maw of the stove, he told me that he had timed the main lambing weeks to correspond with Easter this year. In that way the schoolchildren can witness a lambing event if they wish or delight in seeing lambs several days, or indeed *hours*, old, assembled with their dams in the hay-baled fortress provided for them.

On hearing this a countrywoman, who visits regularly, commented on her concerns as an apiarist. She noticed the bees had reduced their hive entrances by 90 per cent to keep their equally sheltered quarters warm and dry. She believes they may have answered to a collective instinct that yet more inclement weather is to come in, which, on the last occasion, occurred in the winter bridging 2009 and 2010 and was particularly severe.

Apiarists noticed, as the winter loomed on the horizon, that many bees were out collecting nectar in unbelievingly large numbers and agreed that a 40 to 45 minimum of jellied honey was needed for what appeared to be a normal winter on that horizon. This year seems to have been normal so far; but are darker days ahead?

## Wollaton, Nottingham

In this time of so very gradually moving away from the winter solstice, if one is not an agriculturist, forester or professional gardener very little seems to be occurring and here in Britain we tend to regard the winter as dragging on.

We cannot see, envisage, the growth that is taking place beneath the earth. Seed growth. Seeds by the billion on the average farmstead germinating unseen in the great, frozen surfaced womb of the earth's stomach. But the seeds are there, as are the bulbs, pushing, thriving, struggling for warmth when the earth becomes too cold and wet.

We see tree traceries. Whippy thicket branches, silvered by frost or victimised for days on end by the snarling onslaught of the prevailing winds.

If, like me, one leaves home in darkness on these mornings one hears robins singing beneath the quasi-welcoming glow of sodium lights. The best as yet that the commuting hours can offer.

The shadow of a blackbird startles one. Near famished, perhaps hunger has forced it from the roost – sheltered if possible – where it has been roost locked since 4.30ish the previous afternoon.

I scatter grain and bird food in the lane below as I walk, while realising that birds offer more to the seasonal eye in these depths of winter simply because, whether in sodium or daylight, they are around and have to be around in order to survive.

Returning to my flat one mid-morning with supplies, I passed the sitting-room window, here on the second floor, glanced at the red-berried haw thickets and saw four cock blackbirds perched on the thicket crests.

Once I had put the food in the cupboards I returned to the window, my interest being in the positionings of authority taken by each blackbird intent on guarding a storehouse of berries. Through binoculars I focused immediately on a bird that I had never before seen in close-up. A ring ousel. A cock bird perched as if resting and unconcerned by the guarding attitudes of the three cock blackbirds, each perched apart and from window pane viewpoint. The ousel was well to the fore, 20 feet in front of my flat window. My past glimpse of ring ousels had occurred in a well-known habitat of the species, here in middle England, the lower slopes of the Staffordshire Roaches. They have been paired. Cock and hen bird worming and turfing side by side. Regrettably, I have never heard a ring ousel in song. How does the song compare to that of the blackbird, mistle and song thrush, I fall to wondering?

The singleton perched on my thicket top that morning was resting and possibly digesting food, the winter berries it had claimed.

The species in general are known not to be so wary as blackbirds when perched high, and this individual was no exception. He was relaxed, not on the lookout for a raptor or giving the slightest avian regard for the excitable cock blackbirds which obviously recognised him in the context of a rivalling species.

The strengthening sunlight was kind to me in showing the pale fringings on the ousel's wing, fringing thus, to my eye, giving the bird an attractive yet scaly wing pattern. The all-distinguishing broad white breast band flared like freshly fallen snow and the buffish yellow bill, black tipped so it appeared, lacked the brightness of the bills unwittingly sported by the contrasting blackbirds.

My camera was tucked away in the bedroom wardrobe. By the time I retrieved it the bird would probably have flown, such is the way of the world I figured. However, still perched without feeding, the ring ousel remained for a further nine minutes.

Living on the level with tree branches has distinct advantages, even in the winter. And my visually close berry thickets bring in other interesting species, fieldfares being high on the list I write with a touch of triumph seething through my veins. The arrival of these northern thrushes this far inland depends on the severity of the weather; not so much the gales as the snowfalls and hard frosts which keep the snow fairly well solidified and the top layer of earth beneath it frozen. By this time in the seasonal cycle anyway the insect- and worm-devouring birds of the summer have become the berry-plucking birds of the winter.

Leaving in the pre-daybreak chill and darkness one morning for the city and its coffee, national newspapers and necessary shopping, I returned home still relatively early in sunshine following a snow coating and barely glanced at the thickets as I trod carefully by in outdoor boots. Two floors up and I was looking at the silver birch stands and the thickets glistening in their winter 'willow pattern' traceries, while reflecting on the feeling of peace that spiritually swathes the flat like a well-fitted carpet, when the 'chacka-chacka-chak chak' calls of fieldfares shattered the silence. On the roof and soon to come down to the berry thickets obviously, my train of thought advised. Soon to come down to the berry thickets, yes. But about a dozen fieldfares were much closer than the roof. They were, in fact, perched in the willow branches almost hiding from view the suburbanscape from my kitchen windows.

The fieldfares and I were settled on our respective perches at about the same level. The entire outer window space was filled by fieldfares all facing the same direction – west – and perching on and amongst the network of willow branches.

How close could I get before they flew? Had the window been wide open those framed so obligingly within the glass could have hopped onto my kitchen table.

I relaxed my approach at 4 feet and the experience was that of sharing a same willow branch with the fieldfares. And the bird closest to the window *must* have been aware of my proximity. But surely, I mused, it could not have been aware of the glass barrier fitted, years ago, so strategically into the space between us?

Had the glass pane not prevented it I would have contemplated stroking the plumage of that closest fieldfare, beginning with the nape being softly tickled by an extended forefinger. Only in close-up can we really appreciate the different plumage and covering textures. The greyish blue head and nape, white broken stripe above the eye, its pupils projecting a curiosity of liquid depths. The dullish yellow bill, the crop, belly and undersides flecked with linear patterns of brown and in shapes resembling arrowheads. The unique almost deep vulpine brown of the upper wings with brown narrowing into the blacks of the wings' primaries and coverts. The blueish grey merging into black ending of its tail. Blueish grey, brown, the fieldfare may well be described at distance but a close-up is needed to really appreciate their feathered evolved artistry.

As one body, and for no reason that was apparent to me as the lane below was clear of passers-by, the fieldfares arose harshly chattering but merely settled on 'my' thickets and began their singular pluckings of berries; a characteristic of the thrush tribe, and in contrast to the starlings which hover close to berry bunches and attempt to collect three or four berries at a time.

Wintering thrushes, such as the fieldfare and redwing, share with waxwing – a member of the starling tribe – a tendency to remain in one location for several days if a good natural food supply, such as berry harvests and orchards with ground layers where fruit is rotting below the trees, is on hand.

Each bird appears to draw its own 'food larder' map within its head. Yet each flock is governed by the uncanny, *unequalled*, avian mode of flight synchronisation in which observers such as I are left speechless and wondering when an entire flock of birds lifts into the air at almost the same second. Redwing, the smaller northern thrush, occasionally accompanies fieldfare flocks although the species also flocks but in a less guarded way than those of the fieldfare.

Redwing are pert, colourful and, to my seasonal eye, ever on the alert. They flock, yes, but space out more among themselves than fieldfare.

All such wintering birds flying down from the north roost in the relative warmth of our coniferous forests.

Their seedling droppings, probably also dispelled by blackbirds, often take root despite the surrounding acidities created by the mosses and pine needles carpeting a forest floor and, given the light, embryo haw and blackthorn bushes can occasionally be seen thriving among and below the pines due to past generations of northern thrushes having roosted there.

Until I came to live here another winter visitor, the waxwing, failed to visually delight me unless I went in search of these birds. However, due to the occasional extreme cold spell, they fly in – sometimes 20 to a small flock or grouping – and settle to feed 20 feet from my windows.

Waxwing are unmistakable, especially when viewed with the sun on their plumage. And how they enhance the comparatively dull and lifeless winter thickets.

Although related, the waxwing is slimmer than the starling. The cockatoo-like plume on the head is yellow-gold in colour, the eye is surrounded by a black patch and the throat is black but with a higher patch of white dividing the throat patch from the eye patch.

The body plumage is pinkish or fawnish grey but the black and white barred wings, along with the 'head crest', as I think of it, leaves the observer with no doubt about the species framed, preening or swallowing berries in his or her binocular vision.

The adult birds display tiny red projections, almost like daubs of paint or plastic, on their secondary feathers. Wax, as originally described, and how, of course, the name derived otherwise, in my opinion, the species could well have been called 'a golden-crested starling'.

Waxwing display a tolerance of human proximity *providing* the human is moving or walking by or below their feeding thickets. Within each feeding group there seems also to be a lookout, a self-appointed flanker, should a small raptor suddenly appear on the scene.

Finally, regarding the 'body clock' of all these winter feeding birds, they always appear at around the same time in the human derived day at a certain thicket or feeding station while they remain in one location. Not infrequently they will visit a berry thicket twice in one day as if they are doing a round-the-clock food intake marathon.

The earth is offering them energy and they must take it accordingly. To ignore this offering would mean that they were unable to survive.

## Serpentine, Hyde Park, London

Despite the persistent chill created by the overnight frost I persevere with my habitual Saturday morning cappuccino and sip it al fresco style beside the Lido.

11am and frost still rimes the tabletop here where I'm sitting.

Shooting across the span of the Serpentine a hen sparrowhawk homes in so close that I have no problem in seeing, although momentarily, the brown and white underparts and barred tail. Her assault on the Lido building is intentional. She views the structure, and correctly, as a gathering place for house sparrows and pied wagtails. Thus she sweeps in with legs lowered and talons extended ready to grab and strike down in a remarkable turn of speed that will undoubtedly end the life of one small feathered victim which conserved its energy while roosting cosily last night in order to feed a predator this morning.

## Holme-Next-the-Sea, North Norfolk

Inland the countryside is snow locked, yet here at midday the sun is warm and the sea, for all my lack of nautical instincts, looks inviting.

About a hundred great crested grebe in winter plumage ride the incoming tide, each group of individuals diving in unison as they search for small fish and crustaceans.

The beach is deserted. A flurry of snowbuntings rising in low flight resemble snowflakes caught in jet streams and unable to settle. The sky is flawless blue, the sand surprisingly warm to the touch.

## Welney, Cambridgeshire

From the spacious hide maintained by the Wildfowl and Wetlands Trust, I home in on the pools kept free of ice due to the waterfowl and their persistent searchings for food according to the species.

Fortunately there are diving duck here, tufteds and pochard as expected, alongside the colourful shoveler drakes dabbling with the relatively demure ducks to which they are paired.

Mallard preening on the ice, although to many regarded as everyday birds, revert to a sheen of splendour when the wan sunlight takes on those green heads, crimson fronts and blue speculums. In fact, even the greyer back feathers become enhanced in such light to the extent of me focusing with the camera, just as every visiting bird artist is hoping that he can repeat the colours in his or her head in readiness for the palette.

In truth I am here to study the behaviour patterns of the whooper and Bewick swan groupings, get my whooper swan 'fix' for the year.

Intentionally flooded in some parts, these vast tracts of water and meadow green islets – the Welney floodmeadows – serve the same purpose as Slimbridge, Gloucestershire and attract in family parties and flocks of whooper swans, the majority of which inhabit the Icelandic regions during their brief summer breeding seasons and migrate, as instinct demands, to the west and southern hemispheres before the long winter months set in. These are the birds of legend and quasi-instigators of mythology.

We outdoor writers tend to go into realms of paragraphs relating to distance, travel and wilderness when we are enthusing about whooper swans. Personally I'm more in favour of tracking them with a device, but, yes, the variations in land and seascape over which they fly creates a sense of great tracts of wilderness *and freedom* within the most perceptive and romantic of human minds.

Through the Welney observatory's telescope, however, I intend to watch the behaviour patterns of these large, relatively straight-necked swans. And which, so far as them seeing the upright figure of a human traversing their summer fjords and lagoons, thus putting them to flight or, if they have cygnets, on the defensive, can truly be regarded as *wild swans*.

In the fields around Lakesend and Ely groups of whoopers are to be seen grazing in the manner of cattle or sheep. But on my few outings this way I have never seen them within 40 feet of the roadside, although local residents may claim differently. What swans make of vehicles I haven't the faintest idea, but from these grazing locations they come into Welney off the drains and fields and enhance each telescopic scrutiny, for me at least. Only on one previous visit here have I been disappointed in that the swans, both whooper and Bewick, were far out from the observatory and that was in December 1998, according to my notebooks.

That year there was a record number of wintering swans in, the warden informed me. Some 1,200 whoopers and 1,800 Bewicks. But on the day of my visit they were en masse and grazing on the floodwater, well out of comfortable viewing range.

Leaving in the 4pm darkness, our headlights emphasised the monochrome effect, as they scoured the sides of a long roadside drain, the effect being created by a busking or displaying mute swan drifting on the drain's coal-black water surface.

More recent years than those have provided some memorable close-ups of whooper and Bewick swan groups however.

The larger of the two flat-winged swan species, they are what we are aiming for so set the telescope accordingly. More yellow on the bills and those throaty trumpet calls. The majority here are in family parties, the two or three cygnets bearing now, in their first winter, swarthy grey necks and wings. And their bill tips are dark pink with whitish pink taking over the masking between the bill base and the beady eye.

Notice the long neck, the elongated-type head and, in the adults, the black-tipped bill with the deep yellow of contrast. Excitable in that they call communicative fashion as if vocal contact is an evolved asset for their survival.

In close-up through the 'scope notice how they face each other, wings flapping and crop almost to crop, their beaks agape thus revealing narrow tongues such as are seen in the mute swan flocks when they are hissing at dogs.

By contrast the large goose-like whoopers are noisy, their calls varying in pitch, but the so-called whoops or trumpetings never ranging from the basic 'hang ang ang ang' or 'clock clock huk huk huk huwk'. But, yes, I think you will agree that the pitches evolved due to these outbursts do vary.

When they arrive on these wetland meadows, or traditional feeding grounds as perhaps we should best describe them, then we humans know that the ice is forming en masse across their northern breeding and summer feeding grounds.

Like all the swan species aquatic plants form the basis of their diet, but here in England they graze almost exclusively on fieldgrass and, like the mute and Bewick swans, also on acres that have tenanted sheep.

Sheep leave the pasturelands greasy and as this 'grease' resembles the oil fluid that swans and other waterfowl store in the body and spread over their respective bodies for use as a waterproofing agent, the swans are attracted to it. Indeed, at short range, they may even smell it.

But, sheep pasture or none, the swans gather in the daylight hours to graze grass, winter wheat and, again, soils that have, the previous season, harvested acres of oilseed rape.

The main breeding zone of the whooper swan population which winters here in Britain, and I believe some parts of Ireland, embraces Iceland and northern Scandinavia. Also included is the USSR and on across the so-called Siberian wastes. The only enemies appear to be the varied species of fox across their extensive ranges, although perhaps wolves and wolverines. Nests had sparsely been recorded in southern Greenland by the 1960s. But, *infrequently*, pairs are said to have bred in Scotland.

October is the recognised month for whooper swan migration and a warden at Welney recalls standing gazing into fog cloaking the autumn wetlands and hearing the calls of whooper swans erupting through the grey screen as, undeterred, the skeins came into Welney to begin their wintering season.

While moonlight is, of course, beneficial to overland fliers like swans, many ornithologists believe that the star patternings or 'paths' are of greater importance.

Once settled, different groupings and families fly out to explore other feeding grounds, much in the way of the mute swan. They may remain within the core centre of an unseen abacus but explore every extensive arm that the abacus has to offer, simply because they need to feed. Wild geese, while perhaps roosting on the sea and coastlines regularly, explore that abacus pattern in much the same manner and return to the sea, coastal marshes or reservoirs to roost at night.

Returning to the telescope and the behaviour patterns of the whoopers ensconced within its lens, the sight of whooper and Bewick family groups feeding brings outlying families in, to equally capitalise on the flooded over crop or grassland if they can force the tenanting family or *families* aside. There is much squaring up to each other; cob to cob, pen to pen. Standing, wings flapping and, in a scant few instances, seriously striking out with those wings while honking. If one family manages to eject a rival family, or indeed a non-breeding group or cygnets of previous years, a cob and pen sail side by side gyrating their necks and posturing as best as their portly bodied structures will allow. The cob, in particular, imposes his dominance and ensures that the small family unit are aware of his flocking positioning within the assembly.

Adjust the telescope so that you can watch this family coming in to settle on the tract of water immediately in front of the observatory. Note the wingspans, of the adults in particular, and the easy flight rhythm and slight tippings to one side of their bodies as they poise to plane down on the water, with short legs stiffened and paddles splayed to give them full seaplane-effect momentum.

A dominant cob, and occasionally *the pen* of a dominant cob for that matter, will make use of its feet or paddles when it planes down. He or she ensures that they splay, *hit* the water and create a staccato clapping sound.

Again I read this as a sign of power. The cob, as you may already have noted through the lens, is drawing attention to himself, and indeed the respective presences of his mate and brood.

But the cobs of the whooper and Bewick species are not the only swans to be using their paddles in this way. Our resident mute swans, if they hold, or intend to hold, dominant positions, also use their paddles to display dominance. They will also use them if they are pursuing one of their own species overland or along a stretch of towpath, or having clambered up a shallow weir to the stretch of water above. In front of the mute swans that may be assembled there, the dominant cob will clap his paddles forcibly onto the weir sill as he walks and will be displaying arched wings at the same time. When he lowers his keel into the water, the non-breeding birds will move away. Not swiftly, unless the dominant cob chooses to pursue them, but gradually thus denoting and awarding the dominant cob with the respect he is demanding from them.

But returning now to our family groups of whoopers and Bewicks. They feed, preen and oil and fly together in a tight unit. The cygnets of the previous summer will return to colder, but wilder, tracts of Sweden, Russia or from wherever they came. But with their parents. However, they will be driven off the natal territory, and in most cases permanently, when the cob and pen begin again to breed.

Those families which have fed to the fullest are preening and oiling on the green banky islets now. Amongst them are those attempting sleep, their heads and bill tips turned back into the scapular feathers. If focusing allows, try homing in on the eye of the nearest bird. Notice how it closes the eye for perhaps ten or fifteen seconds at one time, then opens the eye. We humans may refer to this as 'cat-napping' and I doubt that birds, species that are vulnerable to predators, sleep in the sense that we humans do unless they are on an island and fully aware of the fact.

Pretty well exhausted or incubating swans are sometimes taken by a fox but, by and large, the majority remain safe, self and family guarded.

Those noisy family rival affrays that I have previously described, we must remember are new to us but occur within the whooper and Bewick flocks several times daily, in fact more often than we realise. The Bewick swan, if you look closely at one or other congregated and 'up-ending' for grain here in front of the observatory, differs from the whooper in that the Bewick is the smaller and carries, as an adult, less yellow on the bill.

This species is breeding resident of the Arctic whose migrational route at the onset of autumn takes it across the southern Baltic to western Europe, which includes Britain and parts of Ireland. Skeins and family groups appear to have their migrational routes imprinted within the instinctive workings of their heads. The same can be said for the whoopers.

Migrating Bewicks stop off to feed and rest, probably at the same location each migratory season, although there must be exceptions. For instance, in the early 1970s, 24 came into the deer-park lake at Wollaton near Nottingham where I live. Although they stayed for one day, they did not repeat the following year. Nor have Bewicks settled here since, so far as is known, although they have been seen following the course of the River Trent three miles to the east. But, again, I stress not on a regular basis, and winters pass when Bewicks are not recorded at all.

Portly in appearance, individuals vary slightly according to size, sex and genetics in the same way as the whooper and mute swans. The territorial claims and displays of aggression are similar to those of the whooper.

In front of the observatory down below on the feeding pool, the three swan species congregate, although remaining wary. Studying them here you can revert from telescope to your more familiar binoculars, which will also provide close-ups of the pochard, tufted and wigeon ducks swimming and diving for submerged grain and potato particles, just as the swans are rooting with heads and necks submerged for the same fare.

Due to the breeding season being several months away there is not a deal of ferocity taking place, although aggression has not entirely waned, amongst the male individuals in particular. Outbreaks of fierce fighting are rare. But passing skirmishes, a dominant whooper cob and dominant mute swan cob snatching as they pass, are more discreet and then only occasionally are you likely to witness these suppressed displays of ferocity.

It is a well-known fact here at Welney that the truly wild swans – the whoopers and the Bewicks – have only to see the silhouette of a human being on the floodbank and the entire assembly of them, or near to it, will rise noisily and fly several hundred yards away. Yet they will accept one human wheeling a barrow loaded with grain and other fare here in front of the observatory and spading grain onto the water alongside both the barrow and the Welney Trust's warden. These feeding sessions take place around deep dusk or sunset dependant on the cloud structure but is usually between 3.30 and 4.00 at this time of year.

Oh, look at those! About forty long billed wading birds, bar-tailed godwit, rising from across the pools and islets and making for the Ouse Washes. Something's put them up, although, to be honest, I didn't realise they were out there in the first place. Small waders have taken off too. Snipe, dunlin, grey plover, too far out to say at this distance.

A bird sweeps in from right to left. Little raptor. Which is why the godwit took off.

Merlin. She has perched on a snagging branch of that dead tree, look, but I suspect will eventually glide over to a fence post by the peripheral drain. *She*? The dark brown wings and head top and mottled below, with fawnish grey feather patterning conspicuous against the white, endorse the fact. And note, too, the square-ended tail. A male would be greyish blue on the back wings. The wing tips would, like those of the female, be black and the tail darkish grey.

The darting, sometimes close to the ground, flight arrangement of the merlin excites me. I love the speed, coupled with the capacity to strike so strategically.

At first glance, especially in this fading light, that merlin could have been taken for a fieldfare or mistle-thrush. Yet at – what…? – two hundred yards away, those godwits recognised it immediately and, as usual, had taken off as one body.

Were whooper and Bewick swans ever domesticated and used as a source of food? They were certainly recognised 40,000 to 42,000 years ago for the peoples of the last Ice Age, particularly in Europe, used the slender, long and hollow bones for flute making and, where possible, made five holes for each of the musician's fingers to coordinate.

The USSR had long prized swans as birds that could be hunted and, indeed, commercially farmed. The entire subject of swan farming is subject within itself. Consequently, there is little space for discussion in the next few paragraphs, but suffice to say that the farming and exploitation of Bewick swans, in particular, ceased only with the outbreak of the Second World War.

From the times when swan bones were used as tools, the pinions or flight feathers as quills and, in Iceland, the feet as purses, swans have also been prized by furriers. Hand muffs were fashioned from the skins, for which the dressmakers of titled ladies' attire charged highly. The soft downy skin and outer skin was sewn into scarves as well as muffs, and a cured swan skin scent was included in ladies' gift scents, which included scented bags or reticules, and were either carried around by hand or in the overcoat pockets of the well-to-do wives of both politicians and prominently placed businessmen.

I was once shown the cured skin of a Bewick swan which had remained in a family for at least three generations and was purchased on a London market stall.

As I expected, it was still silken to the touch many years later. The chin and throat skins of deer, particularly red deer, were cured and prized in much the same way.

Welney now at feeding time. The water in front of the observatory floodlit and a single Wetland's Trust employee venturing out with the food barrow and, with the spade, ladling good-sized quantities of grain out on the water, which is quite literally besieged by waterfowl, most of which are wild in that they have never been touched by humans and, speaking for the majority, will remain so.

My friends and I do not stay for the floodlit spectacle if fog creeps in across the fenscape. It is then that we get out onto the road for home. But if the weather looks to be clear then the feeding hour at Welney can be truly rewarding.

# FEBRUARY

## Church Wilne, South Derbyshire

In a sheltered corner of St Chad's churchyard – seemingly without a community in the sense that it is situated between the Trent and Derwent floodplains but serving only the parishioners of Breaston and Sawley if they choose to travel out – flowering snowdrops enhance the winter layers of beech leaves. The short snowdrop season has arrived, along with the lambings and early daffodil clusters.

Robins twine, snowdrops flare white on otherwise winter-darkened soils. Goldeneye drakes exorcise their elaborate courtship displays on the private fishing water beyond the churchyard rear wall.

Well-drained but slightly moist soils serve best for snowdrops, the roots of which nurture an inner strength of survival that sees them pushing onward with their winter's end progress even though the ground layer may be carpeted with frost or snow. And that is what I, personally, find so remarkable about them.

As I may indicate in later paragraphs, I love natural survivors in any form. And snowdrops are entirely evolved survivors. Yet another species said to have been brought over by the Romans, these splendid flowers really won the interest of those Britons born around the 1850s, when the Crimean War provided many families with anything but solace.

Dependant on when, where and how they are planted, snowdrops can be flowering before the early crocuses and are probably in their peak flowering numbers throughout February. They begin to peter out, display-wise, around the middle of March.

The experts tell us that the snowdrop clusterings need separating due to their botanical resilience, and the common snowdrop, *Galanthus nivalis*, which I think we have before us here, loses no time in outspreading, hence its name.

This variety is recognisable due, first, to an examination of the leaves, which are narrow, and the head singular flowered. The leaf colouring in a good light and close up, if an opportunity permits, is greenish grey.

The flowers of most snowdrop species are between 12–15cm, and there are about nine different varieties.

The lean, smiling and weather-coated man who walks the Draycott and Breaston footpaths 'at least five mornings a week' is really clued up on snowdrop propagation. For instance, when transporting his snowdrops in the sense that he takes them out to friends for replantation or variety exchange at a garden centre, he uses sodden newspaper sheets or kitchen towels dampened to keep the roots moist for it is important that they don't dry out.

Garden snowdrops need to be divided every two or three years otherwise too many flowers will be competing for the rain and sunlight and not a few will suffer as a result of colonisation.

He waits until the flowers begin fading. Snowdrops, which are notorious for drying out, are best planted in the late spring and not, as I used to think, in the autumn.

When the foliage at winter's end and the beginnings of spring becomes withered, then this is the best time for replanting, some 10–14cm below the soil surface and preferably in groups of three. That way they gain build-ups of moisture throughout the rest of the year, whereas autumn-planted bulbs, many already dehydrated, fail to gain the benefits of the natural water, dampness, warm soil and nutrients that near year-long planted bulbs best survive on.

When, after two or three years, the snowdrop beds produce the appearance of a 'bed' rather than a display, it is time to divide them. Thin them out and re-establish them in the garden.

Making one big uprooted clump into two or three clumps should be a practice not to be frowned upon, and on replanting in the recommended early part of the year give them a good watering to rebed them in. The footpath walker here in the churchyard with me today then halves all the remaining snowdrops and replants them 6cm–8cm–10cm away from the original clump.

Out across the lane – a bare patch of ground which also serves as a car park for the people visiting St Chad's Water – there was once a farm and roadside barn, he tells me. To here he was taken on summer dusks to watch the barn owls leaving just ahead of those bygone or 'hay wain' sunsets by his father, just as I accompanied my father out to listen to the unique hooting of tawny owls on the walks closest to *my* home.

Ageing though we are, the footpath walker and I, we are both lucky in that we are members of a pre-computer generation and were awarded parents who enlightened us upon the whys and wherefores of the natural scene extending immediately beyond the windows of the respective houses in which we lived.

## Staines Reservoir Nr Windsor

Divided by a walkway, this reservoir is the centralised area for local birdwatchers in a region flourishing with early established gravel-extraction lakes and ponds of all shapes and sizes. The surrounding fields graze winter store cattle and, at the time of this visit, donkeys.

The green mushroom shapes of anglers' umbrellas line the banks throughout the season I'm told, and so stocked with freshwater fish the reservoir resembles a huge aquatic bowl. It is not a large blot within a waterscape but more an aquatic bowl standing on a ledge of concrete.

Out there today, on the wind-furrowed surface, rides a black-necked grebe. After diving and ultimately feeding on its food intake living below the water, the grebe fluffs out its plumage, possibly to dry in the wind. I can think of no other reason and it doesn't need a graduate in zoology to be working this out.

Through binoculars we watch the grebe using its bill tip to comb and straighten the barbs of its feathers, its neat head used as a fulcrum or feathered cogwheel so effectively shaping each feather, *the barb of each feather*, into the much-needed pattern of perfection that the bird recognises within itself and fills we observers with the awareness that, *indeed*, birds have bigger brain working capacities than most of us realise. Every bird appears to know the barbing arrangement of every feather in the same way as we humans know the shape of our own fingernails.

Out there on the wind-ploughing expanse of the reservoir the grebe could, at first glance, be taken for a floating black cushion, but a *velvet* cushion, as it spreads out so efficiently and rides the flow which is its home.

The profile describes a steep forehead and the feathered suggestion of a double crown. Yet, again in profile, the back of the skull appears sloped, which curves gently down into the length of the neck. The bill is short, pert. The eye, when enhanced by streams of certain light, gleams red and the black pupil within appears, by comparison, to be so tiny.

The throat and cheeks of the black-necked grebe in winter garb are white, yet in summer are black. The neck is sooty grey. The upper wings, in the individual before us, still resemble a cushion as the grebe continues preening. But the tail is white and resembles, to the human eye making comparisons, the saucer edge contour of a rubber dinghy.

Below the water surface the grebe is known to be a snatcher and swift swallower of insects and minnows. In the winter the insects probably live close, in a state of near torpidity, to the stems of the parent plants. Consequently the grebe will probably take in some listless leaves and a small section of plant stem during this hard season.

As many as seven black-necked grebe have been recorded feeding here through the winter months. A friend recalls, in October, a kestrel flushing a wheatear from the shoreline here. Although the kestrel pursued the wheatear in no haphazard way, the smaller bird found refuge in a gorse thicket.

There are, as expected, tufted and pochard duck diving and preening out there. A small concourse of shoveler dabbling duck by comparison, resting bill tips into scapular feathers, on an island. A greenshank, streaky plumaged to the point of resembling a wind-blown tuft of long grass at distance, diligently searches the far side shoreline.

## Virginia Water, Surrey

Later the same day. The 'great estate' atmosphere of oak and horse-chestnut trees, lakeside deeply planted rhododendron thickets. The treetops are peopled noisily by a bird species which are listed as 'pests' hereabout for they are so many and, according to the residents, 'so noisy'. They are ring-necked parakeets, former residents of Iraq but now introduced into Belgium, Holland and Egypt as well as England where they are by no means popular so far as I can ascertain.

In the autumn they thrive on beech mast, of which the Surrey treescapes hold pleasantly many. In the winter, and not surprisingly, they colonise suburban birdtables and nearby patios.

Presumably they roost in evergreens because their plumage, at first light, seldom appears dishevelled. A researcher tells me that they also roost in reed beds and can be seen in good numbers around Datchet Reservoir and Wraysbury Reservoir. These waters, along with Staines, were once the ornithological hunting grounds of broadcaster, television anchorman and naturalist the late Kenneth Allsop. His outings in these parts, during the 1940s, '50s and '60s, provided the background for his 1949 published novel *Adventure Lit Their Star*, an account describing the lives and movements of a pair of little ringed plover, a species which Allsop first picked up in his binocular vision in 1947.

The first breeding pair in Britain were recorded in 1938. But, who knows, little ringed plover may have been breeding here before that time.

The novel, incidentally also featuring a notorious egg thief and a naturalist out to thwart him, was further published with revisions in 1962 and again in 1972.

What Allsop would have made of the now locally described 'hordes' of ring-necked parakeets I could not hazard a guess for they roost apparently in his once beloved birding zone.

Several decades my senior, Allsop as a personality always remained out of reach but appeared in the *Tonight*, and other, programmes in our sitting room when Jean and I were young parents.

As a personality I found Allsop riveting. In this, the twenty-first century, however, it is I who would have wanted to interview Allsop about the many changes that have taken place in this area, especially since the Windsor Safari Park days. And the ring-necked parakeets would have been high on my list of questions.

On that particular visit I also watched a flight of 18 mandarin duck rising from the surface of Virginia Water. Mandarins, as I'm due to relate in later paragraphs, are as new to my seasonal eyes as the parakeets. Again an introduced species originally from Asia – through introductions and due to full-winged birds leaving wildfowl collections established by the landed gentry between the two world wars – Mandarins are now considered a free flying species which breed hereabout.

In foreground silver birches, a greater spotted woodpecker explored tree bark in a bid to extract and feed upon torpid insect life. A flurry of long-tailed tits joined it, intent on the same quest. Sixteen I made it and, as the ornithological field guides remind me, not really titmice but a maverick species and unique.

As winter flockers, long-tailed tits may move across sections of a country in search of food but for the remaining three seasons of the year are considered to be sedentary. I love hearing their songs emanating from stands of April blackthorn, and the quick 'eeerr' calls of alarm, neither of which is given out that day but should have been because in less time than it takes for a human to bend in a bid to tie a shoelace a hen kestrel, a strategic russet-winged avian terror, descended upon the group. Pert-tailed baubles, they rose panicking but the kestrel grabbed one in mid-flight for both birds. A tiny shower of bird feathers momentarily graced the path of the wind as the kestrel bore off with its warm and still living burden.

Seconds later a small flock of siskin flew in to plunder the cores of an alder stand. The entire afternoon's sightings had to do with food and feeding. Such are the demands of February.

## Brayford Pool, Lincoln

Where the neck of the River Witham snakes between the 'olde worlde' tourist attraction known as 'The Glory Hole' before entering the bygone Roman port of Brayford Pool, the mute swans file over the water surface to join the concourse already gathered at the bridge from where they are fed.

At the entrance to the pool, sitting the water surface and facing outward, are a cob and pen in full 'busking' display. Their drab orange bills indicate birds of a good age, maybe 30 or 40 years. And they may also have been together for that length of time as a pair, if not an incestuous breeding couple. A state of affairs which is by no means uncommon in any mute swan fraternity.

What gives me this impression is the fact that these are both larger than average individuals and, therefore, were the offspring of a similar strain. They may even have been hatched from eggs laid by the same parent couple but be a year or two apart in age. There are, however, not many years between them, and by more than coincidence they are probably closely related.

As the flock members file by them, the pair identify or put them into age categorisations according to the colours of their bills.

As yet the pair have not expended their respective capsules of energy on the younger flock members. Those which have dusky grey or black bills they display little interest in because these are the cygnets hatched two years ago, or less. They do not yet prove a threat to the adult couple which are there to display their dominance, their self-elected high positions regardless.

Those passing swans with pink bills, unless a young cob chooses to challenge the dominant couple, will also be allowed by. For these are three-year-olds and again, under normal circumstances, will respect the high positions of their elders.

But should a red-billed cob appear at the Witham's neck and be displaying or 'busking' to impress the equally young pen at his tail then the situation is fuelled by the mature pair who immediately regard him as a rival and possible future contender for their breeding territory, which will be situated within a three- or four-mile radius of the place where Lincoln's swans have gathered for the winter.

Creating a wave of water as their paddles are geared into action, the pair surge out – a white avian warrior and his lady – in a bid to send the younger pair on their way but also make them aware of their lower-ranking status. At least compared to the self-considered rank they hold themselves. They will attempt to snatch at the wings and necks of the younger couple and put them into a skittering subordinate run through the water.

Mostly a dominant pair are successful in achieving this unchallenged display of flocking status. But not always. Very occasionally a young pre-breeding cob, eager in the avian sense to impress his mate and fuelled by early season testosterone and wellbeing, will turn and fend off his older assailants. Sitting on his tail with paddles acting as walking water supports and wings outspread, he may well face the cob of the senior pair similarly offering battle and a full wing-flogging assault could take place. But 70 per cent of these affrays end with one, the youngster in most cases, withdrawing and sailing in the wakes of the passing others with his waiting mate or intended mate.

Why does the normal affray usually end quickly? Because, although testosterone may, at this season, be running high with both cob swans, they will dislike having their plumage tugged and possibly their wing feathers displaced. Once clear of each other, the skirmishing combatants will dip their bodies below the water surface, roll and get as much water over their upper bodies as possible. Next they will rear several times, sit on their tails and shake the surplus water from their plumage. If they have been grabbed by the assailant in one particular place, the cobs will divert their cleaning and grooming attentions to that place and, in human terms, appear pretty well obsessed with getting every feather or layer of down back into perfected order.

Both cobs will next select a preening place and, with arched wings moving in the shuffling fashion, preen and re-oil their plumage. If the elderly mature pair sail from the Witham's neck and beach to preen on the streetside ramp of Brayford Pool, members of the assembly already preening there will move aside for them. Should they not, however, they will be bullied into submission. The old pair will grip their necks, lunge at their wings and generally trounce the subordinates until they make a space for them. And that space is usually sizeable, the mature pair make sure of that. Neither cob nor pen will preen and oil with other swans touching them or even within a neck-stretching reach of them. Thus more plumage pullings, neck nippings and wing grabbings take place amongst them, and if they choose to remain on the ramp and not enter the water the subordinate will be almost touching the swans closest to them.

On this occasion the younger cob, flapping and circling while sitting on his tail, his bill agape and momentarily hissing, withdraws and submits to travel with his intended mate the water trail to the bridge taken by the files of foregoing subordinates.

The mature pair, still with their wings arched, face each other crop to crop and turn their heads both in tandem and unison. In all probability the cob will thrust his head and bill tip upwards and give out between three and fourteen trumpet notes. They will then await more of the wintering assembly sailing round into, or leaving, the neck of the Witham.

Eventually a single cob, probably a temporary widower, sails into the Witham neck. He too is arch winged. He too is a large individual and around the same age as the dominant pair. To my surprise the pair do not challenge him. Nor does he baulk on seeing them. Probably at this time of year the trio pass within feet of each other every day. But one thing I *do* know, all three know each other as locally gathering winter visitors on Brayford Pool.

They may even be members of the same brood hatched locally those many years back. But they would have become rivals in the breeding seasons and establishing their positions at and on recognised territorial border lines: a stand of bankside willows, a bridge, drain or sluice entrance. The cobs, while their pens were on their respective nests incubating, may even have fought. Who but a local swan enthusiast – and they exist in every city – could say?

Today, however, the threesome show no animosity and the widower, assuming that he is such, sails on towards the bridge. Have the dominant pair now ceased their combined harryings of the subordinates? Not a bit of it. As another file of youngsters sail into Witham's neck, the dominant pair surge forward like pale Viking ships threatening war. Thus the situation will remain until hunger induces them to sail down to the non-breeding flock, still maintaining their positions, to feed on endless bread and pastry scraps thrown from the shopping precinct row of bakers and confectioners.

Such is the avian way of things.

# MARCH

## Welsh Border Country

Despite a burst of mild weather at the beginning of March, the barometer plunged overnight. By morning a raw easterly wind accompanied the grey daybreak merging over the Shropshire Hill country through which a friend and I were driving the ten-mile-long ridge of the Long Mynd. The Stiperstones, exposed to sky and weather south of Mynd Ley and Wenlock Edge extending east of Church Stretton to Craven Arms, were white over with snow.

Parking in a layby, I decided to photograph the aspect of bleakness by focusing over a low stock-proofed hedge and ditch but saw nearby a tubular farm gate looped with pink twine. This, I decided, would serve just as well. Beyond the gate, but close to the bare-stemmed hedgeside, stood a sheep, a ewe of the Clun Forest strain. She was on the defensive having, only hours before and probably during the snowstorm, given birth to two lambs. Still stained with afterbirth about the ribs and saddle, one lamb attempted to stand, swaying uneasily, its head bobbing and eyes, though large, appearing unable to focus on the wind-stirred hedge branches holding its attention. Bleating weakly, the second lamb struggled to its feet, scrap of wet tail wagging as the ewe stepped alongside it. The lamb was about to find the teat and feed upon the colostrums that contained the protective antibodies all lambs need as a kick-start to their future.

The first lamb staggered a step or two over the gate, trampled slurry churned up by Land Rover and tractor. Swiftly the ewe nuzzled it with her muzzle. The lamb instinctively pushed the muzzle through the wool of her sides and flanks before finding the entrance to the stimulating fluid.

Speaking softly to the ewe, I moved along the hedge over wet chilled grass because she needed to be relaxed – if animals ever do relax in the human sense – in order for her and the lambs to suckle effectively.

Down the sloping field stood other ewes, the majority with lambs. More than one, I surmised, had lain with her head lifted skyward and groaning as her straining forced the water bag from her system. The nose of her offspring and its fore hooves had then appeared and the lamb had slithered out into the chill, saturated by mucus and afterbirth, to become soaked yet again by the small hours' snowfall.

Among the ewes, humped like islands across the freezing pasture, were straw bales, each positioned in the shape of a cross and against which the ewes and lambs could seek shelter from the wind.

It was then I saw the dark upright movement; a lone man walking. A farmer or shepherd out on his lambing rounds which, in some cases and dependent upon his marital circumstances, could extend over several 24- or 48-hour periods.

Born probably within this inhospitable terrain, during winter at least, this man had probably nursed the first immature lambs of the season, and as he walked the length, breadth and periphery of the field he met with the ewe that had given birth beside the gate.

From a distance the man – the farmer, stock man or shepherd – appeared to be walking firmly. Once one is actually walking over a terrain of grass greased by the bellies of sheep and interwoven with light, thawing snow, the truth hits home just as one's heel prints sink into the ground. One is actually taking a step forward and two steps back or sideways, body bent a little to take the strain. A hazel or any kind of stick is one's best friend in such circumstances, along with the cattle dog weaving wolf-like from each set of hay bales extending across the field.

Without meeting the shepherd, as from here on I will refer to him, I knew that he was hardened to the weather and healthy because the lambing season – as with almost every aspect of farming life – demands that much of a man or woman. He was also aware that his ewes were fit in the sense that they could give birth without complications. Overweight ewes provide those complications. As he reached each newly-born lamb, the shepherd would check its mouth and nose and clean them of mucus. He may also check that, minutes after struggling to its feet, each lamb is seeking the ewe's teat.

A modern-day shepherd could, at first glance, be taken for a casual hill-walker because he or she usually carries a rucksack or canvas bag attached to the shoulder. In the bag will probably be a powerful torch or flashlight, thermometer, disinfectant soap, a short rope to aid a ewe experiencing a difficult birth, bottle of iodine for 'midwifery' or cleansing the lamb's navel, a towel for the shepherd's hands and a large tube of coloured spray. This he will spray on to a ewe and lamb, using a corresponding colour as a flocking aid to ensure they are not separated.

Unlike the average city or suburban dog owner, he has long acquired the ability to stop or redirect the cattle dog by using a single word. The two work together. Every city or suburban dog owner in Great Britain should be made to see this and adapt accordingly.

The shepherd undoubtedly had hay bales in mind for shelter with a stockpile of hay, oats and mineral feeding blocks stacked in a relatively dry barn or stable.

There was no sign of a farmhouse. Nor could I detect a wisp of chimney smoke to pinpoint its location. But there would be a porch somewhere in which the shepherd abandoned his muddy boots and entered the inviting, perhaps even obligatory, farm kitchen with the comforts of its Aga. Yet several more hours of tramping the lambing fields may well pass before he reached that kitchen, the smile of his wife and welcome mug of coffee laced, no doubt, with whisky, I surmised.

## Wisbech, Cambridgeshire

Flat countryside on a dawning of overcast skies dominating all beyond the windscreen. Hedgeless fields.

Vast, tramped by land-dependant and hardy countryfolk, even to this day.

From midsummer until the autumn, these fields blaze golden with grain or ranked with acres of dark green leaves as potatoes, cabbages and sugar beet thrive within them.

Beneath the soils the remains of a once great forest await the light in the rows of oddly soil- and peat-transformed shapes, which are actually tree remains known as 'bog oaks'. That term, however, is used broadly because not all the trees have been identified as oak. There have been other species. However, all are thought to have succumbed at some stage to a subsidence drop of cataclysmic proportions which brought in the almost legendary floodings, allowed peat to take hold and render villages and settlements to become horrifyingly cut off from each other.

Thus conditions adverse to the needs of the humanoids were formed to become geographically known as The Fens. Any modern-day name throughout the area that ends with the suffix 'ey' or 'ea' denotes such a place which the suffix endorses in Old English as an island or islet. Here the element-hardened generations of people survived on the best that these great stretches of watery waste had to offer. Many lived an entire lifespan and knew nothing else, or nowhere else. However, the Romans raised a causeway and created drainage channels linking their garrisons.

In the thirteenth century a drain or 'cut' was dug from centralised Peterborough to Guyhirn. This 14-mile waterway diverted the waters of the River Nene then and still serves its original purpose.

A Dutchman, Cornelius Vermuyden, a drainage engineer in the time of Charles I, was then assigned to drain off all the water. His first attempt was thwarted due to the royal purse lacking the money to pay the workforce Vermuyden estimated would be needed.

The second attempt proved successful and the canal called the Old Bedford River was constructed, to be followed and completed in 1649 by the New Bedford River.

The general idea was to get the water flowing downhill out to sea and not have it return with the encroaching tides. Consequently sluices were *eventually* set up and maintained. Yet the tides and the rains still had their way, though, of course, to a lesser extent.

Nevertheless, the efforts of '*near natural*' plan were considered a failure, long term and poorly serving.

Thus the idea for pumping windmills came to fruition and proved successful. I should add that these windmills were not set few and far between. They were established by the *hundreds.*

Today the problem could still arise, although the windmills have been replaced by electric and diesel-driven pumps, and The Fens produce vegetables, crops and flowers, more so tulips, but also great farm-produced areas of daffodils.

This early Saturday morning, row upon row of local folk, or one would think of them as such, are bending, kneeling and cutting, in small armies per field, as they carefully reap in the early daffodil harvests, which, by Monday, will be displayed on market stalls throughout the region. A person has to love the land and, indeed, the flowers to be hardened to such tasks for which there seems no easy way of extracting each stalk carefully from the soil.

Rain slants down. The Fenfolk are weathered, quite literally bent to their tasks and undaunted. They live with and close to the water as they live with the soils, the scents of peat and the great formations of cloud that, soon after daybreak, will lift their genial and determined spirits or drench them.

The daffodils they are harvesting are propagated. But daffodils were recorded thriving wild in the woodland glades of England during the sixteenth century. But I know of no one who claims to be a horticulturist to the extent of confirming whether or not daffodils were *introduced* to this country.

There is possibly someone out there, at Kew Gardens or the Oxford or Cambridge Botanical Gardens perhaps, who could provide an answer, *endorse a claim* of a sighting beyond the sixteenth century. But research though I have through piles of old books, I cannot locate data regarding the daffodil before that time. And I *do* have to move on in life.

Daffodils to the passing seasonal eye are just that. Long stemmed, carrying sunbeams on each of their petals and shaped trumpet-wise as if they had been machined in a factory.

They lift the spirit, encourage you to put the winter out of your mind and think – *and look into* – the weeks ahead. One daffodil variety that must regularly be seen braving the snow wind is called 'February Eye' and with good reason. In April there then arises a fragrant species carrying the name of 'Old Pheasant's Eye'. Nor should we ignore the smaller varieties. Diminutive or miniature daffodil types are better able to withstand the adverse weather conditions than the taller-stemmed varieties. I delight in seeing them in bloom around the boles of trees, particularly the silver birch. They also enhance a shrubbery, pathside border or any corner of a garden which would otherwise have little to offer. At least so far as the human eye is concerned.

At the close-to-home garden centre I am shown the variety called 'Jack Snipe', graced with a yellow trumpet, and 'Jeffire', a variety which has deep yellow petals and an orange trumpet. In the past I have planted these in my garden borders without knowing, or indeed giving a thought to, their name or variety.

'Jenny' belongs to the same family. Its petals are creamish white. They are bred from a parent strain that display long trumpets. The strain is known as *Narcissus cyclamineus*.

To my mind the seasonal eye prefers to see daffodils clustered green-stemmed, golden-petalled and planted in the colonial sense with space between the flower.

Daffodils are, in fact, narcissi but with long stems and large trumpets. Neglective gardener, though I describe myself as being, I loved in past years digging in holes with a trowel to plant the bulbs. Holes, as recommended by a horticulturist friend, that should be three times the depth of each bulb. Such care, which I likened to putting a newly-born baby into its cot and tucking the covers just cosily around that little body to keep it warm, prevents the frost from damaging the bulbs.

In mid-December 2015 daffodils lined the Derbyshire roadsides of Risley Hill. They were in full trumpet display but five weeks earlier than normally expected. And, yes, they could be 'February Eye'.

Heads of flowering daffodils contrasting with, and relatively high above the snow, have become subjects for the weather photographer in present years and are today displayed in accompaniment with the weathergirl or man on the evening channels of most local television centres.

Cornwall is known to be the county where daffodils come earliest into flower and, with one recent exception, are usually showing by the middle of December. That one exception, however, proved to be a rich flourish of Cornwall daffodils preceding the weeks of early winter in November 2015.

Again this surge of welcoming flowers took advantage of the warm air streams filtering in an incredibly mild weather flow when the Met Office recorded maximum daily temperatures of 3.8°C above the month's average. Indeed, the beginning of November 2015 proved to have been *the second warmest* since 1772 when the first meteorological records were established.

Winter, to my mind, incidentally extends from 1 December until the end of February. People shudder when I mention this and exclaim, "Yes, but what about March and early April?" And while there is much truth in our experiences of raw winds and icy drenching rains occurring during these months, I have known robins, dunnocks, rooks, ravens and mute swans to be nesting within a week or two of St Valentine's Day. I have also known the first mute swan egg of a local clutch to have been laid on 8 March, and the behaviour patterns of rooks give me the impression that first eggs are up in their nests also by that date.

Daffodils at that time we not only expect but take delight in seeing. Yet, as the late autumn-early winter period of 2015 has proven, if the conditions are there so the plants take full advantage of those conditions.

Every quarter or so mile along these Fenland roads flanking a dyke or drain, a singular mallard drake can be seen. He may be preening and oiling on the roadside grass bank or dabbling on the water surface.

If you can slow down your speed, notice, if the road width ahead allows, that there is a stand of brambles fronted by reed or sedge on the opposite side. In there the duck will be incubating and well camouflaged. An often sizeable egg clutch beneath her reliant upon her body heat will be doubly heated by the down, the 'brood patch', plucked from her crop and interwoven into the nest.

At intervals the duck will join the drake for a feeding and bathing session on the water. They may also take off swiftly and excitedly and beat a superb aerial display over the fields and drains in the immediate vicinity. A third or fourth drake may join them and compete for the duck's sexual favours. But if she is incubating a full clutch she, on landing, will cover her body with her wings, tighten herself while giving out a series of clucks or quasi-quacks in vocal rebuke. In all probability the established drake of the pair will drive the outsiders clear of the scene, and aggressively.

Even the Fenland drains are truly alive at this time of year.

## Nottingham

When I was around 11 or 12 years old my mother, sensing my boredom perhaps because the dark nights were in and I couldn't venture far, used to suggest, on an occasional Saturday or Sunday evening, that I went to the off-licence for a packet of crisps and a bottle of Dandelion and Burdock cordial.

On the five-minute walk home with the bottle of cordial tucked beneath my arm I realised that, when the cordial was handed to me in a glass, I was in fact about to swallow the liquid ingredients of two plants. So far as I was aware both grew in the wild. Of course, dandelions I was well acquainted with but burdock I would fail to recognise without a handbook. I used to think then of hops, plants or crops that I had not seen but which I had heard were the main ingredients used for making ale and the alcoholic liquor beer. Malted barley distilled resulted in whiskey. Sloes or the berries of our blackthorns were used to make gin. Rose hips could produce a syrup. The list was endless. As a species ourselves, then, we drink plants.

We also eat them – plants and crops. And meat produced, we believe, by grass.

We also smoke them and clean ourselves with varied concoctions made by them.

Plants of the past we use for heating, and it should come as no surprise that we wear them as clothes. The fibres from jute and similar plants imported from Bengal we use to make sacks and matting.

Flax, the blue-flowered plant that we boys saw growing in the fields during the Second World War, and the seeds of which are called linseed, is cultivated for its fibre which is used in textiles. Consequently, during wartime, it was used for manufacturing parachute ropes and straps.

Plants and flowers have long been used as dyes and, to some extent, in modern-day body art.

To scientists of the past, plants seem to define an explanation. We take pleasure in seeing them. We *enjoy* them. They bring beauty into our lives. Beauty and colour. We view them in a wild state or propagate them. Set them out, *garden* them for our own individual purposes. And now, as a species, we farm and cultivate them. Indeed we *parasite* them probably more than is generally realised.

People, scientists and specialists in the medical profession, have, through decades of experimenting, discovered – like the old bygone countryfolk insisted – that many plants and flowers nurture healing properties. But why? And why do they apply so strategically to the human race, the temperate wilderness farmer and explorer. I am referring now to the drugs that, in many cases, heal us. Codeine, aspirin, morphine. Digoxin is used for slowing the heart, Vincristine and Taxol are used as anti-cancer agents. The bulbs of daffodils have, in comparatively recent years, been used in the production of Galanthamine which may yet prove beneficial to memory loss.

Reading the ingredients, *the compilations*, on the side of a packet or tube of healing pills can prove fascinating. One wonders if, in the future, more plant or flower extracts will be added or some withdrawn.

We make journeys out to see specific plants and flowers. We photograph and draw them. Or we are just contented to stare but *enjoy* them visually. Yet, as far as survival and general wellbeing is concerned, we now depend on them more even than when our ancestors were trekking and hunting in the forest or tundra country within proximity of permanent shelter, or a labyrinth valley offering the shelter of caves.

In many instances we are living longer, tending to our ailments and benefiting more than we realise due to the evolution of plants. Could we exist without them any more than could the bee? Sometimes I wonder.

## Stratford-Upon-Avon, Warwickshire

Midday with sunlight striving for recognition between morning-long banks of clouds. Meridian, at its weakest as yet, I muse while crossing the Avon at Seven Meadows Road Bridge. Once over the river I descend into Mill Lane, with interesting buildings on either side and a glimpse of the Avon's weirs, before I close in on the Holy Trinity church, where some remains of the Bard are believed still to be buried.

As the sun finally breaks through, a mistle-thrush begins tuning from an ornamental cherry tree. Noting a public seat, I make for it because I simply want to sit and listen, not to a staged recital but the meandering notes metered out by this interesting, early nesting species. The cock bird up there in the leafless branches has staked out a territory, possibly attracted a mate due to the persuasive notes of his repertoire and is also warning off several territorial rivals at the same time. Particularly if the rivals were hatched on the territory.

The opposite side of the river provides a 'worming' meadowland habitat for blackbirds, song and mistle-thrushes. The wide acres of grassland are their communal dining table. And the shrubberies and thickets around the weirs and the Holy Trinity church provide all they need in relation to shelter, roosting and nesting quarters. What the sightseers make of the lone man sitting on a seat in this tourism-enshrined corner of the churchside I have no idea. Nor do I care. They will have to make him what they will. In truth he is here listening to the swelling and varying overture of a bird that has not yet appeared on stage. At least not today, for him. The song of the mistle-thrush carries much less of the flutings created by a blackbird or the repetitiveness of a song thrush. To many listeners it is probably the least attractive song of the three. Perhaps because in his ramblings, which are by no means weak in deliverance, the mistle-thrush seems to be feeling his way rather than rigidly keeping to the orchestration and following the baton of the conductor. Nevertheless, his notes are clear-cut and here by the Holy Trinity church they re-echo along and around the buildings and courtyards on either side of Mill Lane. The effect is akin to that of performing in a recording studio equipped with a top-quality echo chamber.

Instead of one bar of song, the ear perceives three. Rambling, yes, but unique nevertheless. And, although there is but one mistle-thrush singing here in Mill Lane, the visitor, or indeed a local resident, could be forgiven for thinking there are three or four.

I love the old name of 'stormcock' the old countryfolk bestowed upon the mistle-thrush. He sings high and into blustery weather – literally *facing it* on some occasions – the cloud mass, the downpour of rain, the freezing drift of a sleetstorm.

Once his territory is staked out at the end of winter he needs everything and everyone to know. So the lone man on the churchyard seat he is a visitor, yes, in a sense. But he is not venturing along The Shakespeare Trail today.

## The Dell, Hyde Park, London

Rockeries, silver birches, orange and purple crocuses, bringing a sense of peace and inner being to the heart, lured me to a seat here. I was due for a rest since I'd walked, *A-Z* in hand, from a publisher's office in Museum Street and included on my way to Victoria the chain of Royal Parks.

St James proved a seasonal revelation since the willows on and around Duck Island were clothed in the most glorious swathings of young foliage, like green velvet, with the sun striking them so strategically against silver spurting cascades of fountains.

Up through Green Park the sense of an approaching new season was not so prolific since there were fieldfares and redwings exploring the turf, as there had been when, earlier that day, I bypassed Marble Arch. But The Dell in Hyde Park also shared a proportion of the key bunch which, at the appropriate turning of the earth towards the sun, would unlock the door to the new season.

Seconds after me sitting, flask fished swiftly from the rucksack, a mistle-thrush cock thrust the overture into life. Between each outburst of song, the mistle-thrush pauses in his deliverance as if he is selecting which bars to come next. The pauses, however, are shorter than those of the song thrust, the song itself carrying slightly less throaty exuberance or, to the human ear, sounding more as if the mistle is finding his way as I noted earlier with the songster at Stratford-Upon-Avon.

A dunnock tinkles briefly, and blue and great tit pairs whisk by in their undulating flight patterns. The time of year has arrived when every one small bird becomes two. A pair. And where one goes so mostly does the other. It is as if they are joined together as pairs by an invisible thread.

The obligatory robin appears at my shoe end. I toss him a crumb or two which he snatches up quickly. In flies a second, its mate, which waits in the background.

The first is the cock bird. Seizing a crumb he hops briskly across to the hen and presents it to her. She solicits, opening her gape and shuffling her wings as both robins did when they were youngsters. Once she has swallowed, the hen bird reverts to the pert trim shape which flew in originally. She allows the cock bird to feed her in this way for some minutes. It is a form of bonding for this species. Probably for all small passerine bird species.

Over on a rockery display, a wood pigeon pair sit 'ala preening'. 'Ala' means touch and the wood pigeons are certainly doing that. With their short pale bills, each of the wood pigeon pair preen the down on the cheeks and nape of its intended mate. Jackdaws, and possibly other 'corvidea' species, indulge in long bouts of it, often until they are disturbed by an *incoming* jackdaw.

To we humans most bird species look the same. However the behaviour patterns, which, with the early singings, begin at this time of year, the impression, *the visual message*, that a human observer receives is that of certain male and female gaining internal 'bumps' of pleasure on seeing each other. Thus the birds are attracted and become attached to the point of pairings and eventual matings. Thinking along these lines, I needed to leave The Dell and head on along to Victoria Station. Could I rise without disturbing the robin pair? Would my shadow, which birds cannot work out, send them flying back to the shrubbery? Admittedly they hopped a little aside when, with the mistle-thrush cock still singing, I took a step or two around the seat I had just vacated. But within seconds the little cock bird was again presenting his 'love' with cake crumbs which, her open gape and shuffling wings informed me, were gratefully accepted.

## Welney, Cambridgeshire

A few hours spent observing the behaviour patterns of the whooper and Bewick swans before they leave for their breeding grounds.

Usually the main body leave around 13 to 15 March, the lengthening hours of daylight having their effect on the migrational urge by this time.

The journey taken by the Bewicks covers some 2,300–3000 miles. There will be 'short feeding break stops' along the way. Time needed for refuelling. And when they arrive a breeding pair, if they still have their cygnets with them, will need to chase those cygnets off the nesting territory unless, like some pairs, they retain them for a further year, then breed in the April or May following.

At the time of their departure, usually daybreak if the temperature retains a crispness or the contrastingly secure promise of thermals and isobars suitable for their journey, I wonder how the swans determine between the need to be flying from feeding ground to feeding ground here in the English Fen country or heading on the long journey to their feeding grounds of the Baltic. But of the adult pairs I believe the instinctive pull – the final decision in human terms – is made by the pen of a pair. Family party after family party are probably motivated into flight by the excited calls and restless consistency of the other swans – Bewicks or whoopers – taking off around them.

The smaller Bewicks are more angular in appearance than the whoopers. The bill patterning is also an important recognition feature an important recognition feature between the Bewicks and the whoopers due to the yellow colourations in the latter's terminating in a sharp angle, whereas the termination point on a Bewick's bill suggests a rounding off as the patch skin levels with the first bevelling of facial down. A whooper's bill carries more yellow than black. The skull shape is angular. A local taxidermist measured a whooper taken into his workshop for skinning and arrived at the measurements of 65 inches for a cob, whereas the female is probably less by about 10 inches. That particular bird, for, like the mute and Bewicks, individuals vary in size, carried a wingspan of 108 inches, which I consider exceptional in having experienced 81 and 84 inches as those of an average-sized whooper cob.

At whatever time of day the observer records the skein flights of whooper and Bewick swans, he or she can consider themselves to be witnessing a skein-borne spectacular. True, a member of any large waterfowl family cannot dive or expertly and suddenly swerve, but the directness of the flight, coupled with the formation and occasional interchanges of a wild swan skein, is seldom, if ever, taken for granted even by those whose occupation puts them alongside these intriguing birds daily at this time of year. Usually we observers see wild swans flying from an elevated position and at any time of the day, although daybreak, around meridian if the light is exceptional, clear and beckoning, and at sunset seem to be motivating flight factors. I would think that more are seen at sunset around the area known collectively as the Ouse Washes, than elsewhere in England and Wales, because they are flying to feed on the contents thrown from the grain barrow wheeled in front of the viewing hide at Welney. Many of these swans display hunger tactics even though they have been grazing out on the fields around Upwell and Lakesend all day. But grain to waterfowl is addictive, and good thing too, because it aids in swiftly refuelling them and replenishing their fat reserves, which will be refuelled probably on less protein fare as – in the case of the Bewicks – they make their way over to their Baltic breeding grounds.

When a swan pair take off – either from land or water – whether mute, whooper or Bewick, the cob usually sits displaying his readiness about 1 foot aside and back from the pen and it is she that makes the first foot-running, wing-flapping move across the water surface. The cob follows two or three seconds later, and if one gets a chance to study swans in flight – either passing overhead or from a photograph – one will see that the pen, frequently the smaller of the average pair, is a head and slight upper foreneck ahead of the cob. In human terms, then, it is *she* that makes the final decision and her mate, her protector, that follows, as do the cygnets of the past season.

However, if a cob disproves of the place in which the pen chooses to plane down for feeding and grooming, he will give out a series of low barking, almost whickering, call notes, and the pen will usually respond by flying on until they arrive at a feeding ground that is amicable in its location to both. I have seen this happen twice with flying mute swan pairs and once with Bewicks.

Whooper and Bewick also 'gaggle' talk, but briefly, when families or pairs are flying. But not at all on a seemingly regular basis in the way of wild geese. I have seen at least one photograph of Bewicks in flight in which the pen has her bill agape and is presumably 'talking'.

The journeys made by whoopers and Bewick are today closely monitored. But, personally, I'm quite taken by the fact that the swans continue flying for so long and in those inevitable skeins and flight positions just as long as conditions appear favourable. The feeding and grooming stops aside, they do nothing but *fly*. Are they reading weather signs and cloud formations? Their collective heads seem to be clear of everything except their destinations. They have no powers of thought compared to ourselves, yet they have instinctively adapted themselves to remaining airborne in every sense of the word.

They face collisions with power lines, shootings and the threats of adverse weather conditions, but they do not turn back. Although, as already stated, they may take refuelling shelter for a while.

Researchers have now acquired information on the heights travelled by Bewick swans making for their Baltic and associated breeding grounds. In her T A Poyser publication *Bewick Swan*, researcher and professional enthusiast Eileen Rees mentions heights of between 100 and 400m when making sea crossings but when flying overland, if a terrain needed to be well cleared, the swans were aware of and sought higher paths, according to the land mass below. Sir Peter Scott, founder of the now nine or so Wildfowl Trust reserves, recorded flight speeds of 35 to 50mph. He was also of the opinion that they flew mostly at night, particularly beneath starlight. The whooper's range, again according to Sir Peter, takes in Iceland and northern Scandinavia. Skeins range further across the USSR, over the Urals and over and around Siberia to the coast of the Pacific. A scant population ranges still on towards Manchuria.

Here at Welney on this day of our visit both whooper and Bewicks, families or singletons, are excitable to say the least. With heads uplifted and wings flaying air, cob faces cob, pen faces pen, crop to crop and spasmodically striking out at each other with bills agape. If disputes stray beyond that and actual wing-lunging fighting breaks out, actual physical contact, such as body locking, is brief mainly because each antagonist means to keep its plumage, and particularly its flight feathers, intact.

As we are seeing through the telescope here the aggressors at this time – when the migration period of these birds is about to take place – seem relieved to be withdrawing from an out-and-out affray. In the months gone by the disputes lasted longer because feeding group, or family, territories needed to be established, however temporary, and they served each family, singleton or pair.

Looking beyond the aggressors there are those whoopers and Bewicks – probably non-breeding birds – which seem content to be preening and oiling or dozing with necks swung back and bill tips tucked into their scapulars. Obviously they are fully fed or they wouldn't be doing that.

The calls, both aggressive and socially bonded, all three swan species lived with while wintering in their collective numbers at these reserves.

On the water in front of the hide individuals, again of each species, rooted for grain and root crop particles that had sunk below the water surface. They were amicable, tolerant, but perhaps just a *little* spring-loaded regarding the possibilities of an inter-species affray. And *that* would only take place between two birds – males or cobs – of two groupings; and probably end as swiftly as it had been ignited.

Wigeon paddle in amoeba-type rafts around the rooting swans, graylag and pink-footed geese. The whistle call notes of these ducks carry through into the dark hours when, in all areas, the wigeon flocks are on land and grazing together in the darkness.

The fox must also hear the whistles and smell the oily, slightly 'gamey' scents of these duck, which will rise in a cloud once they see the eyes of the fox penetrating the darkness. The wigeon will return to settle and roost on a sheet of water.

Similar to the wigeon in calls and contact notes, the pochard also thread within the concourse of swans, wigeon, gulls and coots. There are many more drakes to the aquatic acre than ducks, the sex ratio seeming to run in proportion with that of the mallard. Pochard can dive deeply but here at Welney need only a relatively shallow water sheet to submerge them as they repeatedly dive to pick up grain and any such small particles of vegetable matter that may have been thrown out of the grain wheelbarrow. The swans are not adverse to having the diving pochards feeding directly beneath their submerged bellies, any more than they are having the excitable wigeon and mallard paddling and swimming around them. It's my belief that whatever species, the swans are aware that the ducks can dive and attack their feet should they make aggressive moves towards them.

In the hide and around the 'scope, birdwatchers identify the dabbling duck species from the diving duck species. Especially if the people are relatively new to bird watching.

When a warden arrives he recognises me from previous visits and remembers that we had both contributed articles to waterfowl magazine 'glossies'. In the past he is keen to tell me that, according to the Wildfowl and Wetlands Trusts records, the number of Bewicks arriving to winter in Britain has shown a marked decline compared to the numbers that were arriving here in the 1990s. There are now almost half of the birds of that time arriving. Obviously power lines play a part in the decimation of large flying birds like swans. But in such large numbers as are missing today? we query in hushed tones and away from the 'scope which the visitors need to use.

Bewick skeins must face storms in which the poorly fed may perish once their energy fats have burnt out and they are unable to refuel due to the harsh conditions. But basically free-ranging human hunters in Eastern Europe and Russia are thought to be responsible.

The *Russian Arctic*, he further informs me, is some 4,700 miles from the traditionally known winter migration grounds of Slimbridge in Gloucestershire and Welney in Cambridgeshire. In a, then, recent survey at Slimbridge, over one third of the Bewicks examined by the staff carried shotgun pellets embedded in their body tissues. They had survived but, nevertheless, were regarded as targets by the hunters, who hit them with shot but failed to kill them.

Climate change and the possibility of Bewick swans finding water plants to feed on in locations on the other side of the English Channel has also been discussed with regard to this halving in numbers. And, only days from now, the Bewicks – both at Slimbridge and Welney – will be returning to their breeding grounds. What the warden and I consider is the outcome when the Bewicks return in the mid-autumn because the skeins have two journeys to make – back and arriving – before we see them in anything like a concourse again. All we can do is hope for the best. And soon after their respective arrivals the wardens at both Wildfowl and Wetlands Trust locations will be counting. Of that fact there is no doubt.

A winter afternoon in 1962. I have a week off work and, therefore, time to spend with my wife and young family. Jean is working in both the kitchen and our little sitting room which, due to the snow out there, is also the children's playground. At least until a thaw sets in.

I have an armchair beside the hearth and am reading *An Eye to the Wind*, an autobiographical work by Sir Peter Falcon Scott. Young working father though I am, Sir Peter Scott's bird illustrations are no stranger to me due to my bookshop browses throughout the six or seven shops in my natal city. There is only C F Tunnicliffe whom I would rate alongside Sir Peter. And now here is a magnificent autobiography of which he must be justifiably proud.

The son of Captain Robert Falcon Scott – who perished on an expedition to the North Pole – Peter Scott served with the Royal Navy in the Second World War. Thus we learn of the warship convoys he experienced in the North Atlantic, his yacht and general boating interests, including as well the crafts of punt gunning.

A gifted artist, Sir Peter Scott founded the World Wildlife Fund and was successful in breeding captive Hawaiian geese at Slimbridge on the Severn Estuary, which was titled the Severn Wildfowl Trust. By 1964 Sir Peter, and his then few supporters – not forgetting his wife and family – were recording the arrivals and departures of the Bewick swans which came to winter at Slimbridge.

As with the mute swan, the two wintering species carry distinctive bill patternings, therefore the researcher is aided considerably. The markings on the bills of our everyday mute swans occur on the underside of the bill, which is why we see them swiftly lifting their heads when they approach each other, especially a mate from which they have become temporarily separated.

Due to Peter and Phylippa Scott's research, we know more about the whooper and Bewick swans than we did in the decades prior to them settling in at Slimbridge.

Peter Scott also made a studio home in his younger days at the Eastern Lighthouse, Sutton Bridge, where the Nene enters The Wash. However, he was not around on the afternoon my father-in-law packed us into the family's little Ford Popular – his wife, my wife, Jean, and I. We were going to a Fenland tract adjacent to the outlying community of Cubbitt, where my mother-in-law had spent some time holidaying with her relatives as a girl.

My father-in-law also knew the local lighthouses, drains and seemingly huge sluices in the Sutton Bridge area and so we decided to combine the areas. Had he and Sir Peter Scott met they would, no doubt, have reminisced about their wartime days anchored on the defensive at Scapa Flow, for my father-in-law also served as an officer with the Royal Navy in the Second World War. The two would probably have conversed about the E boats and the German scuttlings that took place at Scapa Flow during the First World War.

Sir Peter in the Second World War spent two years on a Destroyer called 'Broke'. Whether my father-in-law was on the same ship I have no idea. But collectively, and like many enlisted and nautically orientated men, the two were at Scapa as part of the defensive known as the Norwegian campaign.

Not surprisingly, perhaps, Sir Peter was not at the studio on the day we arrived at Sutton Bridge. A scattering of captive pink-footed geese browsed in the vicinity of the lighthouse. And, so far as we were concerned, that was it. On reflection Sir Peter *may* have been home. But we were not the types to intrude on the privacy of one's home without being invited.

In later years I learned the East Coast poacher Kenzie Thorpe, who I believe lived at Sutton, often managed the lighthouse and its penned geese for Sir Peter while he was away. Kenzie featured eventually in TV producer Colin Willock's filmed series called *Survival.*

Having acquired the skills of calling hares to the camera and, again through calling, coaxing skeins of graylag and pink-footed geese out of the wintering skies,

Kenzie made a name for himself as a coastal guide and understandably charged for his talents and services.

When he was caretaking for Sir Peter at the East Lighthouse, he is said to have posed as his employer and told visitors that, yes, indeed, *he*, Kenzie, was Sir Peter.

Although we missed both men that day that visit to the outer washlands, as I think of them, has remained with me through the years. Such winterscapes have produced great human characters with whom I share the same affliction – which is wanderlust.

## Breaston, Derbyshire

A break in the rough weather of just one or two hours and, like a narcotic dependant, the birds respond by nest building.

By the stockyard outbuildings a robin skims by, settles 10 feet away on a fence post with a grass stem clasped in its bill. Blue tits locate minute mounds of green moss flourishing between the stable flagstones and diligently break them up to be used as the outer lining of a crevice or nest box hole.

Cock great tits reel while the hen birds hurl into hedgebottom grass tufts to seek soft lining materials. In the week-ago snowfall period, magpies continued nest building and, near completing, one pair again positioned their twiggy football of an intended sanctuary in the silver birch branches 40 feet from my window.

A mute swan pair, which mated throughout mid- to late February, similarly brooded over first eggs as blizzard conditions surged in, transforming visually their normally white waterproofed plumage to creamy yellow. At least until the thaw sets in. Once those first eggs are laid the swan will not desert them.

Bird nests of different design, needing different anchorage. The majority camouflaged, some positioned so openly that the safety of them could not be guaranteed, some nests at the mercies of late snow, the majority synchronised to be built when and as the warmer conditions filter in. Nests by the billion, being built, woven or staged as platforms. All serving one purpose. To aid in the procreation of each species and fill any vacuum in the seasonal life throb.

Be aware of those that you can, and, season after season, marvel at the mute beginnings of yet another process interwoven into the tapestry harvest produced by The Great Mystery.

# APRIL

## Trowell, Nottinghamshire

"Look at 'er! She's full of eggs," exclaimed the canal lengthman as he fed grain to the pen mute swan standing on the road embankment of the canal over which roars the M1 motorway.

He pointed to the swollen undercarriage of the pen padding through the grass to the lengthman's proffered saucer and its contents placed at his feet. In a week's time, perhaps a little longer, her place would be taken by the cob for ever on guard duty because the pen would be incubating the full egg clutch in the reedy mound of the nest situated today at a place where the willow catkins flourish, but which was once a wharf used for loading and unloading consignments of lime and night soils and known as Trowell Basin.

Bird eggs. Or birds' eggs, whichever. For a time we schoolboys sought them out. However, at our respective disposal, if we chose to go there on Sunday afternoons, the local Natural History Museum provided all that we needed by way of visual stimulation.

The display cases we had to lean over to look down

into the vast collection of egg clutches, each nestling in an incubational hollow made from cotton wool. So many variations and eggshell designs we enthused; and donated by Victorian naturalists, some of whom took one egg out of each nest, so they claimed, but carefully plundered contrasting egg clutches of the same species on several occasions per outing according to their diaries.

We schoolboys of the 1940s also collected cigarette cards, in sets of 50 per subject, depicting 'British Birds and their eggs' and so not all of the eggs on display in the vast museum cases were unknown to us. Instead they endorsed the cigarette card illustrations beautifully and made each card as important as an encyclopedia.

But when and how long did it take for a bird to lay an egg? And *why* all the variations – some slight, some quite distinctive – in colour and markings? We knew of no book, or museum diorama that could answer those questions for us, even less any gamekeeper or birdwatcher.

However, in more recent years and due to the diligent research of ornithological scientists, our boyhood mystery has been resolved. Or close to it.

Eventually eggs, mating and laying were mentioned in texts by the late James Fisher, and a museum attendant, on realising that we lads were serious in our quests for learning more about bird life, copied sketches and excerpts from a museum library reference book on birds. An Edwardian Victorian author – whose name meant nothing to us – due to his discretion and the word being near taboo in those times, ensured that we never saw the word 'vagina' in actual print, let alone in describing the reproductive system of birds. Had our parents known we had seen the written word we would have been in dire trouble. "Whoever is feeding you with this stuff?"

After the egg is planted as sperm through the vagina it travels along a tight coil which holds the uterus, that, our dictionaries explained, was a hollow cell in the pelvic cavity, and here the foetus womb rests, although the dictionaries were referring to mammals. Nevertheless, we each gained a sketchy idea of what was taking place. And our egg had gained a yolk.

Another new word 'isthmus', describing an unspecified strip, of *tube* in this case, we came upon, and on to the Magnum – all very scientific and not a fieldcraft enthusiast's type of word at all. Nevertheless, we persisted and decided that this was still a holder of the developing egg and which the book told us contained the albumen and membrane of the shell. The entire mystery of evolution hit us on reading this. Seeds, plants, eggs. Evolving. Being made greater than the original cells that produced them. Growing, in our working-class language. Small wonder that the Native American tribes who had roamed and survived on the Great Plains looked upon the entire process as 'The Great Mystery'. Surely the production of a single egg should be regarded as unique.

So the egg, its contents and shell were forming within what the book told us was the oviduct of a bird. *Every bird* laying an egg prior to the period of incubation.

The discovery that membrane and blood vessels were involved served further to heighten our collective beliefs in The Great Mystery. Believe in it! There was no option.

Before the shell and doubled membrane formations,

an egg, I learned, is white. Thus I have the impression of the peeled egg of a domestic hen. The pigments, the blotches, spots and patternings are waiting in the process chamber and are applied between the forming and the laying.

The pen mute swan before me was grain hungry to the point of taking in more body fat and calcium to see her through the 38-day period of incubation. Her eggs are the normal colouration for a mute swan – pale greenish edging into white. But in this species alone variations occur, although infrequently. In boyhood I knew of one mute swan clutch that had, each year, *each laying*, smudges of what appeared to be solidified albumen adhered to the outer shell. And since the 1980s I have known a pen which lays eight or nine eggs a season, but among which two have shells as blueish green as the shells of a dunnock. And to answer the question forming within your mind as to whether or not these eggs hatch, the answer is in the affirmative. They have been fully fertilised.

Eggs are usually laid in the early morning. A friend standing beside the reed bed nest of a mute swan pen gained the impression that egg laying is not an easy process. The laying pen repeatedly shuffled and lowered her body into the nest hollow, while at intervals uttering shrill calls as if in alarm. The whole process, with this species amongst the largest of our British birds, took around half an hour before which the pen rose tentatively from the nest hollow. There were two eggs. One dullish pale green, the second the same colour but shiny shelled. The freshly laid one surely?

Standing over both, the pen proceeded to preen and

tidy her underparts, particularly the anal region. With smaller birds, like the passerines, the process obviously takes a shorter duration. I am thinking of the early morning that I walked a pre-breakfast woodland path with my late friend John Needham and had an egg deposited at my boot end by a flying starling. She was obviously hurrying back to the nest to deposit it but mistimed the process and laid it while in mid-air.

How many eggs are laid from Land's End to John o' Groats at this time of year? How many nests – of *all species* – could a satellite-primed counter positioned as a drone or helicopter record? Its findings would be nothing short of fascinating.

The mating displays of black grouse, great crested grebe are well recorded except that the photographer often misses the *post* copulation display of mute swans, when they tread the water surface, crop touching crop, heads turning in unison and wings beautifully arched. The smaller the bird species the less elaborate the display. At least to the human eye.

We seldom glimpse titmice and finches copulating but to each individual involved in the bonding, the contact of a small bird is as important to *that* bird as it is to a large bird. They experience 'pleasure flushes' in the head on seeing each other, according to satellite or similar fittings and contraptions used for monitoring the pleasure durations of the varied species, including and defining cage birds. And to have the female facing a male is not a sign that they will immediately mate.

Like most humans they need to be attracted. And if

the male of any species displays his superiority over other males, the female searching for the *right* mate makes her presence known to him. Genetically she recognises him as an individual bearing genes that denote superiority, therefore it is through her tapping into this gene line that she can pass her intended mate's qualities on to their offspring.

When the male has recognised that the female is willing, *or striving*, to accept his genes in a sperm sac, the courtship period – the displays and eventual matings – occur. At the height of the display, the male's penis emerges from its sheath and the female parts her wings and presents her cloaca accordingly. Here he deposits his sperm safely, quickly and usually, *but not always*, satisfactorily. In many cases of mating, according to the species, the male has to twist his body so that he appears to almost be underneath the female. This does not apply to large waterfowl species like swans and geese which appear to be riding and half submerging their mate; the pro-copulation displays of geese being particularly noisy, to my ears at least. But, then again, we are talking about large birds.

Cock blackbirds and such flautists sing from territorial songposts. Researchers believe that a male with a good strong voice and varied repertoire is not only advertising the *whereabouts* of that territory but the whereabouts of himself should the passing female find him attractive and, again, make a bid for his genes.

There will be displays of courtship from both male and female for intermittent hours, perhaps several days, before the first mating occurs. And, like nest building, most matings occur early in the day.

Recently the cock blackbird currently dominating the blackthorn thickets close to my window fluted strongly but unseen by me due to the oncoming blossom and foliage. To a patch of grass just offset from the roots of the thicket swept a hen blackbird. To my surprise she slimmed her feathers down and stood with spindly legs braced, her body at an angle of 45 degrees. She resembled a small brown stick or twig, barely more.

The cock blackbird ceased singing. In a flurry of ebony wings and outfanned tail he plunged from the thicket branches and stood in front of the female. Facing her, in fact, but briefly. The prone female outfanned her wings. Swiftly the male hopped alongside her and at her tail briefly connected to her, penis into cloaca. I saw neither obviously. But once he had entered the female he pushed with wings uplifted and fluttering as he deposited his sperm. This last act lasted about four to six seconds. When he lifted clear of the female the cock bird flew back to his blackthorn songpost. The female shook herself, preened a displaced back feather into place, then sprang into swift flight along the hedgerow.

All the foregoing took place in a space of around twenty seconds. Less time than it has taken to describe this account of them.

## Nottingham, North-West

Situated just inside the woodland and green belt zone of the city's north-west boundary, I sit cloud watching a short time before the sunset ignites the sky and frequently see a rotund-bodied game-type bird describing quick beats as it flies purposely towards a habitat and feeding ground beyond my outlook.

For some time I have been unable to identify the bird. Or birds, because there is more than one. But each comes over singularly. Like all such birds, the flyers, each in their turn, are travelling a direct flight line. To and from where? Probably the old wooded duck decoy runnels and pools glistening in the wooded hollows of the deer-park at the bottom of the long hill in the east to the boggy spinney in the fields of Trowell Hall and nearby Swanscarr farm in the north-west. To which, when they are flying, I locate them.

The longish bill is not discernible due to the birds having passed over the rooftops before I'm aware of them. But I have decided that, due to the feeding grounds and habitats to which they are heading, these birds are as English settled as our oak woods for they are woodcock.

Being often these days in the passenger seat of a car rather than at the wheel, I am able to pick out the boggy copses and thickets towards which the woodcocks fly as the driver and I, ensconced in our travelling capsule, make our way down into the floodplains of the Trent, Soar and nearby Erewash valleys.

At the T-junctions of the field and road networks rise – often unnoticed and disregarded – small woods or copses of willow, alder, haw, blackthorn and sycamore intermingled. Within close proximity of a motorway embankment usually. In my case the M1, its grasses sweeping down to the wet fields below because here on the floodplains most of the water was squeezed from its natural swampland when the motorway was being built. Consequently, the fields in pre-motorway days were drier, the streams and runnels since having formed and the field corner copses became flooded because the water needed to harbour somewhere. Snipe and woodcock are aware of these boggy corners, as are moorhens and mallard. And it is to here that I believe my local woodcock fraternity make their to-ings and fro-ings.

Providing there is habitat, however, woodcock frequent these Midland Counties in good numbers and there is no sign of a population decline due to herbicides and pesticides. More likely than not those that fall are shot by keen fieldsportsmen on their shooting weekends, and this has been the situation since game shooting became a popular sport with the upper classes in the eighteenth century.

Northamptonshire I would imagine is a good woodcock county. Here the Nene and its tributaries provide the boggy feeding grounds sought by the species, and although Leicestershire has deep, game-coveted woodlands, where woodcock obviously breed, the field seepages are not as discernible below the M1 embankments because quite a proportion of the motorway in that quarter runs through or over great shelvings of granite.

So far as the sporting gentry is concerned, the appeal of the woodcock has to do with its swift flight, its sudden and whirring rise from a covert, healthy land tract or abandoned duck decoy runnel. Up goes the cry 'cockshutts!' or did in the old days, and the competitive gunbarrels are swiftly aligned in the appropriate direction.

The term 'Britain's largest wader' counts as a misnomer so far as I'm concerned. Fair enough, woodcock wade and paddle but I think to a much lesser degree than they use their feet for unearthing layers of moss, field grass and, as is most often the case, layer upon layer of leaf mould. They are also much at home in tracts of deciduous and forested woodland as they are probing the foggy reed stands in the boggy copses. Moreover they frequently sunbathe, again usually as single birds, in warmed bracken fronds.

To a less gamebird-conscious person than myself, I would describe a woodcock as a bulky-appearanced individual with a longish bill, but not in the sense of the snipe, curlew or whimbrell.

The plumage resembles the leaf layers carpeting the glades in which it forages, more frequently by night than by day. The buff and deep brown feathers are barred, as is the crown to which is added a distinctive black. The throat is buffish, the rump brown and black. The tail is short and rounded, barely discernible to the average observer.

In March and April woodcock are pairing, bonding, as are thousands of bird pairs of all species. We see little of the female. The cock, by contrast, flies above and around his territorial boundary, quite frequently meeting up with a neighbouring woodcock male, an aerial rival to some extent, and occasionally two or three males begin beating, *patrolling*, boundaries together, yet aware of each other. The name we give to these territorial patrols is 'roding'.

When the nights, and ultimately the dusks with them, are drawing out, as we say, roding woodcock can be seen around that time. Some countrymen claim that they can set their watches by them. An example of this a friend and I experienced when we convened at the front gate of George Turton's cottage in the Forestry Commission housing complex beside Sansom Wood approaching dusk hour. Before our interruption George was planting potatoes. Pausing at his task, he glanced at his watch and volunteered, "There'll be three woodcock coming over within the next three minutes." And sure enough the three patrolling males appeared in low, weaving flight, dipping and rising like reconnoitring bats, just as George had predicted.

Roding woodcock do not attain great heights, they are there to make a show of territorial ownership to their equally inclined neighbour. They do, however, take advantage of the green forest or woodland rides and sweep down them in fine style.

I had one roding male pass within 8 feet of me along such a ride, thus giving me a glimpse of its dark oval eye and a rare chance to catch its 'tissick-issick' call note. Due to the positioning of a woodcock's eye set firmly and elongated fashion into the side of the head, I am fairly certain that this bold individual was aware of me. Indeed its intention may have been to see me off.

Standing offside to the main ride while listening to the chorusing blackbirds and willow warblers, I watched that – or other woodcock males – sweeping singularly down the ride several times. An unforgettable experience.

As expected, woodcock nest on the ground and in a shallow hollow lined with grass stems and dead leaves. The eggs, buffish toned but blotched with dark brown, number four. They are positioned narrow end inwards, although the female may alter them briefly around so that they gain the warmth from all sides needed for the chick's development. Because the hen bird sits close to the ground and normally refuses to be disturbed from the eggs, incubating female woodcock, with plumage resembling the leaf layers of the woodland's ground cover, are notoriously difficult to find. The few warreners who do make a mental note – or indeed sometimes scribble out a diagram in their pocket notebooks – of protruding tree stumps, or path tangle of stalks or grass bents, cluster of twigs or log as woodcock nest markers.

Warreners, like my late friend Jim Bark, carried a mental note of the whereabouts of each ground-nesting bird on his patch and unwittingly earned my admiration for his fieldcraft one Saturday morning by pointing out two woodcock nests and a clutch of 14 mallard eggs all within half an acre of the heathland and forestry tracts of Wellow Park in the Sherwood Forest country.

A great young naturalist, Lee Scudder, impressed me further by gently lifting aside tussocks of grass and bramble to show me five robin nests within a patch of around 25 feet.

Lee also came upon an incubating female woodcock that he showed to me and that maintained her incubating stance as we knelt beside her and gently stroked her silken-sheened wings. The hen woodcock remained statuesque, a porcelain model intent on protecting her clutch of eggs at all costs.

The positioning of the woodcock's eyes – which I have previously mentioned – enables her to see such predatory mammals as a fox, stoat or weasel approaching, at which, it's my guess, she may just be persuaded to leave the nest.

Lee incidentally recorded three of the eggs hatching at the nest where we stroked the woodcock but saw a hole in the fourth and remaining egg, thus indicating that the chick had developed to the point of hatching. On breaking open the egg he found the fully developed fluffy chick inside, but a chick for which the efforts of breaking out into the open proved too much.

This strange lack of avian determination is not unique to woodcock, I should add. It happens to birds of all species. But why, since the chick in question has fed on the storage sac of egg yolk and thereby gained a rich source of calcium, does, *should*, an occasional chick fail to make it? That is an ornithological question that has never been fully answered.

A firsts of the season morning this. First willow warbler of the season I've heard singing. First blackcap bubbling from the thickets of blackthorn, burning so white, and each flower cluster unique visually against the flawless blue sky. First tortoiseshell butterfly. First orange tip. And, exploring the frames of my sitting-room window, first trio of honey bees.

## North Yorkshire Moors

Hutton-Le-Hole – Farndale – Blakey Ridge

Wind shielded to some extent by the surrounding moors, Hutton-le-Hole could be described as a showcase village, its fences – painted white – highlighting the contrasts of the grey stone cottages lining narrow winding lanes and two becks swirling and chuckling in aquatic song as they meet beneath the settlement's bridge.

We scale a stile and walk the field path towards Farndale. The immediate fields in the valley bottom are relatively flat and, therefore, easy to harvest. Small woods flank them, then foothills of the moors provide the natural fortress but from which water seepage finds its own long travelled routes and broadens out into the becks and eventually the River Dove.

The ploughland is littered with the corpses of corvidea – jackdaws, carrion crows and rooks – all of which arrived on the furrows to pillage and newly-planted seed. These corpses are probably intended to worn others of the same species off. But do they take heed? Due to the many corpses here I would say probably not.

Where the strip of village fields end we cross the delightful old bridge and, facing oncoming traffic, walk the roadside into Farndale. A cottager or two working in their front gardens nod in acknowledgement but decline to offer anything further which is how I would be if I had walkers and tourists bypassing for six months of the year. I would also feel a little resentful, perhaps giving way to a sense of filtering invasion, if I lived in a showcase location.

At a fieldgate stands a grey, roan-type pony with maned forelock and muzzle raised to accept the titbit that might be forthcoming. This could well be a Welsh Mountain pony. If not, then one of its type. I fondle the rough forelock then move on because I don't feed horses and ponies. It is a practice that is not fair on the owners of these animals because if they fall ill and a vet attempts a diagnosis beginning from their last meal, who knows, if the animal is regularly fed by the passing public, what that meal was?

The Farndale daffodils encompass a two-mile stretch of the River Dove along the opposite bank, there being coach trip weekenders in by the dozens, and understandably. There is a sense of peace and golden or butter-yellow beauty about carpeting daffodils and the sightseers want to stroll rather than set a good pace along the riverside path. Such an adopted attitude, here in Farndale, I can well understand. Slow down! *Enjoy!*

The next one and a half miles take us by the stony building clusterings of Low Mills and Church Houses. On the opposite bank of the Dove a great red bull leaves a drinking bay with three cows alongside him. The cows are competing for attention – his future sexual favours – attracted as they are by the great bulk and the scents of his semen and urine.

When I was a pre-school boy I knew the names and appearance of every bovine species grazing the fields of England. Domestic, and ultimately family, matters, however, pleasantly occupied my 1960s and 1970s years. Consequently, I lost touch with the several European breeds of cattle that were being introduced into this country around that time.

In Farndale I made a rough sketch of the bull, and at the end of the trip consulted an informative little book called *Know Your Cattle* by Jack Byard that I purchased at my local farm shop. The bull was a Limousin, a breed native to the south-west and central massif of France. Indeed decorating the cave walls of the Lascaux Caves in the Montignac district of that country were paintings of cattle strongly resembling the Limousin. Therefore, experts on the bovine species are of the opinion that if these are the Limousin strain being depicted then the cave dwellers of that period hunted, farmed and fed on them. They probably also used them as draught animals.

In that particular region of France, incidentally, crop producing was difficult, and so this great bulky cattle strain was regarded as both a work animal and also a healthy substitute for the calcium deficiencies that might have occurred due to the lack of plants and vegetable tuber crops.

Recognised as a prime beef producer, the Limousin was introduced to Britain with all seriousness in 1971. Jack Byard states that 179 of these animals arrived at Leith Docks, Edinburgh, in the early months of that year. By 1986 the Limousin was regarded as the main beef-producing strain in Great Britain and still holds the record as such.

To our right looms a sandstone massif – a great sloping slab – an obstruction, at the bottom of which a signpost – weathered as the complexions of the ridge and moorland walkers themselves – informs us that 'Blakey Ridge' is due to be served up as the afternoon's main challenge. Our stance, and indeed our gait, changes as we lean forward using our heels and calves on the lowering slopes of this uneven and deceptive ascent.

Silver-haired though some of the ridge walkers may be, they are quick, agile and still managing to converse as they make towards the cloudy en massing horizon. The path is worn and uneven; furrowed, twisting, teasing – your body swings and angles forcing you to use your brain or, in other words, *become a ridge climber*, whether you are used to this type of terrain or not.

The higher we trek the cooler the wind becomes, the darker the clouds. People with sweaters tied around their shoulders or waistlines begin to put them on while walking, *climbing*. Without adequate footwear I cannot imagine anyone feeling secure up on this winding course interwoven with loosely clattering stones and runnels made over long periods of time by rain and sun melt. Runnels that are looking to twist a booted ankle or snag a tendon; unfriendly runnels, challenging.

What grass there is covering this sandstone massif is feggy, unkempt and, to the Homo sapien population, useless. The stones are so variable in colour and size, the pebbles even more so.

Your back! You are having to bend it more. Your knees, that in Farndale you barely recognised as motivators of stance and travel – mere supports in fact – you are now becoming aware of. They are skeletal tools and you are now needing to use them to full effect.

The knee is the second most important bone in the human body, Yet, and especially as children, we take both for granted. However, mountaineers live with the awareness of knee support whether on the mountain or off. Not a few of my mountaineering acquaintances cycle around their home localities. Such exercise keeps their knees flexible and their cartilages in workable order.

There will be people climbing, or *climb walking*, Blakey Ridge wearing trainers. In this day and age there might even be ridge runners. But, speaking for myself, I wouldn't care to have those stone shelvings and runnels beneath my soles unless I was wearing studded or well-trod boots.

Below those clouds, silhouetted against what could be a horizon, is a rickety five-barred gate emphasising the gap in a drystone wall. A goal! Something to be aiming for. That gate. More effort! Come on! Bend that back, lift those knees, dig in with those booted heels. Never mind the gasping phrases of talk, these can come later.

Ah, now doubling your awareness of natural strain are those of your lungs and heartbeat. Working, throbbing but in a lovely sustained rhythm. Imagine your lungs as bellows. Feed them with air, this *cooling* air, for the higher we climb so strangely unseasonable the air streams seem – almost icy.

The farm gate – yards away. Enjoy this next scramble and think just how many people have done it ahead of you. And for years.

Only *feet* away now. Feet… you're touching it, the work of a true craftsman. A five-barred gate. Weather-creased, bored. Up here blind, helpless and at the mercy of the elements. Only we walkers know its purpose and indeed its name. Obviously the drystone wall is a dividing line. A moorland boundary erected at the expense of landowners.

Mosses parasite corners of the stoneworks, grass tufts and bracken fronds protrude from the very cracks that have allowed them purchase but are now screened from view.

Jackdaws, curlew and golden plover occasionally perch, calling, on such walls as this. Peregrine falcons too. And, beyond the wall, have we reached the summit of Blakey Ridge? Not a bit of it.

The ridge is broadly staircased. There is a steeper but, thankfully, shorter climb ahead. So we leave the 'false' horizon and get the climb beneath our boot heels.

Tough going. Joint dislocation country. Slow going because we are having to watch where we place our feet. No point in hurrying hereabout, which lives up to the old adage of 'more haste, less speed'.

Not one of the walkers who were ahead of us has topped the skyline yet. Climbing? Undoubtedly. Occasionally plodding? Most definitely. Becoming bored and wanting a change of scene? Yes, and quickly.

But we are mere animals traversing a natural habitat but, unlike animals, not due to necessity. Why, then, are we here? There are so many possible answers to that question but psychologically I think we have all been looking for, and are now undertaking, a challenge. We can't be mountaineers, but we can be hillwalkers and, hopefully by the end of the day, feeling the better for having hillwalked.

Dammit to hell! Another scramble to a drystone wall which has a gateless gap in it and beyond which is *another* false horizon. You're playing games with us, Blakey Ridge! Are we likely to be off this entire sandstone massif before nightfall? The third horizon proceeds to be the last, that horizon being the sought-after horizon.

Down there is a great shallow bowl of heather moorland, and behind us, particularly above Farndale, a blizzard spreads a freezing sheet across the faintest suggestion of sky.

Here on the ridge summit, by contrast, the sun breaks through. We follow the snake of a descending path, on this occasion now using our heels as brakes, towards the grouse butts.

Rosedale. I first came across the name in the 1970s when reading a trilogy of John Hillaby's walking books. In *Journey Through Love* he and his lady of the time awoke in their cottage 'at Rosedale on the North Yorkshire Moors' to find the cottage pretty well snowed in. Snow, or a small drift of it, had come down the chimney and into the fireplace. Hillaby rubbed with a forefinger 'a portal' in one of the windows to look out on the world of mini Arctic out there. Those paragraphs, and Hillaby's descriptions of the snugness of home, were among my favourites in the book.

John Hillaby? Could one make a living from walking and writing? I silently asked the inside of my head and the silent world in general. He'd written on his walks in Africa and also the, then to become outdoor classic, *Journey Through Britain*.

He had no children unlike myself, who was happy at that time to have two daughters and a son scampering through the rooms of the home with my wife, Jeannie.

So who *were* people like John Hillaby and Gavin Maxwell? When the latter's *Raven Seek Thy Brother* came out and I discovered that he owned a deerhound, an Arab stallion and a powerboat far beyond the financial reach of a Mister Average like myself – who, to this day, depends upon a self-produced income – the fact became clear that they were *both* the recipients of private incomes and probably more.

In later years I learned that Hillaby was born in Leeds and his family – grandparents I think – were the founders and makers of Pontefract cakes.

My second verbal association with Rosedale – which, as we walk this late afternoon, is beginning to take shape like a moorland island in the dale below – occurred in Nottinghamshire. At the Game Fair staged on the Welbeck Estate one summer I struck up a conversation with three gamekeepers. Glancing through the Welbeck Estate gamebooks which were displayed beneath the awnings sheltering one of the stalls, they came across the word 'havier' in relation to deer. No one in the vicinity could explain its meaning.

'A havier', I told them, was the term used for a castrated red deer stag and was in use among the country estate folk from the late seventeenth century until around the time of the Second World War, after which the practice of castrating stags died out. By castrating a stag, probably as a calf, the gentry and their keepers were assured of heavy animals maintaining a good weight of venison when the time came around for culling or butchering. Haviers were kept apart from the usually free-roaming park herds, in three- or four-acre paddocks. And because they were castrated they failed to grow antlers. Thus all the usual calcium absorbed by a stag during the summer months that went into both body and antler development growth, with a havier only the body produced as a result of the natural calcium intake. The result was an exceptionally heavy stag, or 'store of venison' if one chose to look at it that way.

The three keepers pumped my hand and told me that they reared grouse and worked the grouse butt country 'on the moors above Rosedale'. They were warm, cheerful and tanned red by the wind. As we parted they told me that if I found myself in their part of the country to seek them out.

But they are not around the butts as I came down from Blakey Ridge, unfortunately, although there are red grouse breaking from the heather tracts and calling in good number. The calls of red grouse are guttural but fall into a rhythm of quick chattering when alarmed, as the grouse around the butts are today.

A unique tone of russet, they burst through the heather stands seeking seclusion, then peering back and around the stems and outcrops of rock. Challenges amongst their own species and uttered as a means of territorial establishment resemble 'o-ack, o-ack, o-ack ack ack ack' type sound. Those keepers must know them well. Had I met the keepers on the moor today I would ask to be shown, if it is possible habitat-wise, the three well-established types of heather that clothe our open and weathered moorlands.

Ling I am probably best acquainted with. And, yes, it *is* one of the three heather types I have in mind. It is the most prolific of the three growing on acidic soils. The tiny leaves are stiff to the touch and intriguingly grow in two opposing rows along each stem, which, again to the touch, feels surprisingly woody. The bellish-type flowers are pinkish.

On boggy tracts of moorland the cross-leaved heather can be found. The drooping but attractive flowers are rose pink and form in clusters at the end of each stem.

The bell heather bears a shrublike appearance and, again, has a woody stem. The leaves can look green beneath one type of cloud effect and goldish or bronze when seen beneath another. The flowers are reddish or rose pink and most attractive when viewed in close-up.

Like most habitats, heather moorland is today managed and a management technique is to fire the heather areas on a rotational scale because earlier experiments proved that when old heather tracts are burnt the new growth which emerges as a result of that practice is prolific.

The blizzard has remained at our backs as we eventually squelch along the bottom slopes of the moors, with Rosedale – levelling beyond the belt of ash, willow and silver birch – separating the last of the heather fringes, except that we have now a beck to cross. Momentarily diverting our attention as we search for a suitable crossing place is a mallard duck. Having left the nest and covered the eggs with moss and down, she is off duty for a while and anxious to join the drake.

'Tuck, tuck, tuck' she calls in a low tone as if talking to herself. She leaves the beck by the opposite bank and briefly preens water from her underparts before padding, while still talking to herself, through the low, greening vegetation.

The beck? We can either paddle or leap across because the plank bridge is smeared black with mud left from the boots of the walkers who have crossed ahead of us. Patience and a steadying of the eye are needed here. No hurry. It's still daylight. Ah, the beck narrows further along. Leap it? Me too.

Once across we follow the bank line back to the footpath which threads now through the greenery. Slivers of sunlight persuade birds into song. Chiffchaff, willow warbler and cock chaffinch. All now in strong voice. Unseen but perched and singing close by.

Eventually we step out onto a pavement and rows of parked cars, the latter probably having been much less so in Hillaby's time.

The mallard duck has found her drake – immaculate, green-headed and consorting with a babble of other drakes. But he cannot really defend her, though he may try, from being gang raped. The duck indicates that she is not there for the matings by closing her wings tight across her back, where, obviously, a mating drake would position himself, and lowering her head into her neck while opening her bill and giving out a series of quack-type calls that to my ears register as a protest.

The gang of drakes move in. The duck sprints for the shelter of a parked car. She lowers herself beneath it, still protesting. But here we must leave her to seek another parked car – our own – which will take us back to Hutton-Le-Hole and to the second of the cars which conveyed us there.

## Wollaton, Nr Nottingham

Windows open. The scents of 'May' blossom and the liquid peals of blackbird song filling the room. Both potent, especially after rain.

The avenues of the Wollaton deer-park have, for the past week, been hazed with the greens of young foliage. Cock chaffinches join the blackbirds and song thrushes in song. There is a sylvan touch along all five of these avenues yet they have still to complete the foliaged avenue, the '*approach*' scene. This awareness hovers in the mind and before the seasonal eye for around five days.

The morning dawns, however, when, to both mind and eye, the scene reaches completion. The year has returned and the foliage is pleasantly at its fullest. Every leaf of those several billion is open, admitting both light and shade above and throughout the length of each avenue. The teasing question then arises: did we ever know the avenues when they were *not* in full leaf?

If today, as is often implied, youngsters learn little from the natural scene, the majority are, nevertheless, aware that different trees and shrubs produce different shaped leaves. The majority of our deciduous trees compete for growing space, therefore the leaves are broad, or at least generally oval in shape, having evolved to attract in maximum sunlight and soak it up like human beach bathers.

The limes of these English palatial park avenues, along with the leaves like the wychelm and woodland inclined hazel, possess leaves with slender tipped ends and, as my generation at least were taught, evolved with that arrangement serving as a drainage facility through which, after each leaf has taken in its quota of moisture by way of rain, the leaf surface water travels downward and drips off the narrowed end. Should much water remain on the leaves the bacterial plant diseases and fungal decay will take advantage of the situation accordingly.

Each tree species, in the *natural* scene, adapts to the environment to which it is best suited. Chalk, limestone, clay, whichever. Under normal conditions the mountain ash or Rowan will thrive in positions relatively open to the wind. The beautifully arranged leaf sprays carry small blades that appear flexible so far as wind velocity is concerned. Which is why we see them growing, often singularly and sometimes planted by human agency, on hillsides close to crofters' cottages or outlying smallholdings.

Nevertheless, here in middle England – and recently – I have known a Rowan to be split into two by the force of the wind although, I should add, a *very severe wind* with the power to blow pedestrians into fences and even into the middle of a busy road. In retrospect that particular Rowan may have survived had it been trimmed or pruned rather than left to outspray and become a road corner thicket that proved top-heavy.

Avenues, woods, turn green by degrees and according to the tree species planted along and within them. Here in central England we environmentalists have for long come to terms with the fact that the spring, we we know it, begins far south and west of our respective locations and merges north and east as the weather conditions, and indeed the soils, respond to the more favourable conditions that, within ten to fifteen days, are usually awarded them.

Spring. Do we question the meaning of the word? Well, exactly that. Whether plant, bird, animal or reptile, the fit and the able are geared towards reproduction and, in particular the trees, shrubs, wild flowers, crops and grasses, are 'springing' up.

In the deciduous woodlands hereabout, at this season, we are much aware of the 'upper storey' and 'under-storey' in relation to the trees, shrubs and thickets. Many arboriculturists and foresters refer to the upper storey as 'the canopy'. If a tree has reached full height and maturity the leaf spread or canopy occurs comparatively late. But this naturally evolved aspect of coordination ensures that the ground layer, or under-storey, plants and flowers are given sufficient sunlight and the necessary supply of vitamins before the canopy spreads above and blocks them out completely. Besides which, insects need to flourish thereabouts to aid with the various and necessary processes of pollination.

When you sit in a woodland glade, as I am while jotting down these sentences, note which trees are dominant in respect of height, canopy spread and providing shade. These, usually oak, beech, maple, sycamore and black poplar in my neck of the woods, were here before the surrounding smaller trees. They may, in fact, have outlived – albeit *outgrown* – a vast succession of under-storey plants and flowers as well as experienced light-prevailing direction changes due to subterranean movement, caused by faults, and also coal mining subsidence. Basically, then, the mature trees, although dominant, allow for the smaller, lower-storey species to survive and provide pollen at the appropriate times in the entire and intriguing woodland cycle, confirming that nothing, or next to it, in the natural cycle is incidental. As I have mentioned before, the jigsaw's outline is there waiting for the parts to be fitted. And fitted they will be as the year moves along.

Hazel and alder trees can be in flower during a mild February and certainly March. The male catkins resemble buds. These have taken about a year to come into fruition. The pollen-erupting catkins of the hazel have long been known by true countryfolk – albeit *deep countryfolk* – as lambs' tails. Should a breeze sway these catkins, or a bird searching for food settle amongst them, the pollen disperses away into the air.

Many of our parkland and woodland trees are flowering by late April. Trees, such as some beech, ash, silver birch and oak, are pollinated by the wind and, under normal circumstances, remain free of human or animal intervention. The reason is because the trees are tall and pollination takes place relatively high, closer to the crown. Pollen, it is believed, travels a considerable distance.

These, our best-known trees, nurture both female and male flowers. The flowering males are long and appear to be stalk-reliant and dangling sometimes in positions or clusters that look overburdened. By contrast the female flowers are minute or tufting in appearance according to the species. The role of the female is to trap pollen spores blown in on the wind. The pollen, then, incredibly fertilises the inner crown of the female flower called an ovule. Not that every pollen spore achieves its evolutionary goal. It is quite literally a hit-and-miss affair and the misses are in far greater proportion than the hits.

Our beloved English oak produces prime examples of long, downward-hanging flowers but with flowers varying on each branch. The reason why this occurs with most park and woodland trees is because, since they are pollinated by the wind, there isn't a need to produce colourful flowers to attract in insects to aid, by carrying pollen. Denis, an arboriculturist, explained that as a general rule if the flowers hang in clusters from a branch the pollen is scattered by the wind, but if there is a flower – usually colourful or pleasantly and sickly scented, or both – then it has evolved with the intention of attracting in insects to aid the process of pollination.

And *our* eyes see usually only the greening of these trees; the hazes of green to become relatively deep and often widespreading foliage which we take so much for granted once the season is under way.

## Little Paxton, Nr St Neots, Cambridgeshire

With the scents of early flourishing 'may' blossom in the air we pulled in at the RSPB reserve which, at first glance, resembles the gravel-extraction lakes that can be seen silvering the floodplains of any riverine English county. But, be assured, there are some very secluded habitats here, along with impressive stands of thicket to attract the passerine bird species and the incoming contingents of breeding warblers. If a birdscape can rightly be described as 'pretty' then Little Paxton is certainly that. Because, as a young man, I grew up with the awareness that birds can quickly adapt to changing conditions and habitats, the inland colonisation of the once sea-confined cormorant has fascinated me over the years.

The first flight of inland cormorants I saw occurred at, or over, Cropston Reservoir in Leicestershire. The birds were flying from the direction of Groby Pool and heading towards Thurmaston in the Soar Valley. There was no mistaking them. But I admit to my surprise and how out of place they looked weavering in file over Charnswood's hills swathed with bracken and interspersing ancient oaks. More out of place appeared the first inland cormorant – a singleton – which gained the attention of my son – then aged around ten – and I as we birdwatched on a local patch at Netherfield in the Trent Valley near Nottingham. This canny individual had taken up residence within three tracts of water on the north bank of the Trent and roosted on the struts and steel supports of a railway bridge.

On one occasion Stuart and I were there when the cormorant was up and perched as a train came over. The tremor and rumble emanating due to the train's river crossing caused the cormorant – we noted through powerful binoculars – to do little more than flinch. But it did not fly. And apparently neither did the barn owl reported to be often roosting beneath that same bridge.

So doubtful was the recorder of the county's birdwatcher's group of that time when the cormorant was reported by our young friend, the now late Peter Cooper, he journeyed with 'scope and several birdwatcher colleagues to the site. Stuart and I were there with Peter on that particular Saturday evening. Consequently we backed up Peter's report. Further to our delight we located the cormorant preening and wing-drying on an islet. Beside it, to further the surprise, were two shags. Thus began, at least for us, the exodus of these seabird species from their natural and expected sea coast habitats to the inland lakes and reservoirs of the English counties.

At Little Paxton I viewed my first *colony* of nesting cormorants. The pairs were nesting in partially or half-submerged trees, or islet trees struggling to get established. The site warden strolled over and informed us that there were at least *one hundred pairs* of cormorants nesting here and that some nests already contained four young. A cormorant city! I had never contemplated viewing such a great gathering. Especially in my younger days.

Throughout the region, then, must have been adequate feeding grounds and *tons* of fish and the like on which cormorants feed. The Great Ouse flanked one side of the site; long and narrowboats, colourfully berthed, occupied much of the nearside riverbank.

Turning to follow the paths and trails with Stuart, I was alerted to the aerial courtship drama taking place immediately overhead as a pair of hobby falcons wove sky patterns around each other. Narrow-bodied, fast flying, the pair dipped and swooped, in silhouette or half silhouette depending on the light and cumulus formations serving as their background. Each was intent on attracting the other, the whole slender-winged, bird-created sky dance sequence halting we humans in our tracks uttering whatever sounds of pleasure emanated from our respective throats and feeling so confined, fastened on two legs to the ground as we were.

Minutes later Stuart had his 'scope focused on a thicket of flowering may and was beckoning me over. I knew better than to talk or exclaim on my way across to him. There, again, telescopes and tripods are relatively new to the outdoor enthusiasts of my generation. Mounted on a tripod with a tilt-and-pan-fluid head, the 'scope with a quality lens, but which shouldn't exhaust the budget of a prospective birdwatcher, should preferably nurture a high-quality lens, some of which are coated with fluorite.

As father and son, Stuart and I are around the same height and so did not need to move the lens to any noticeable degree. When, smiling, Stuart stepped aside and allowed me into the eyepiece I experienced the almost boyish pleasure of looking in on something intriguing and unattainable. But magnification and the eyepiece on this occasion made both visually available.

I found myself looking into the pink velvet-like encasement of a singing bird's throat and marvelling at the tiny vibration offering of a slender organ serving as the bird's quivering tongue. Moreover, I was facing a singing cock nightingale and an individual undaunted by the shine of birdwatchers' tripods and the anthropoid bulks of the birdwatchers themselves.

How many people had viewed this out-of-the-thicket singer over the past few warm days?

To me, however, homing in on a bird species which may no longer be breeding in my natal county proved an unforgettable experience. While never quite so liquid and flutelike as the meanderings of a cock blackbird, the nightingale's song is pleasant on the human ear, if indeed the bird seems anything but relaxed when producing it. That said, the performance is virtuoso and the trills so rapid and musical and end in a crescendo. The song is elongated. Beginning with 'eeee-oo'-type reels reminiscent of a canary but expanding and is bird-made music of which there can be no doubt.

As he sings, the male moves his head slowly from one side to the other as if intent on proclaiming his territorial domain to bird species other than to which he belongs. He gives out harsh 'weet' or 'chuk' call notes as a warning to his mate or brood should he locate a stoat, weasel or grey squirrel in the vicinity. Nor is the name a misnomer because, in the breeding season, nightingales *do* sing at night, especially just after dusk, as well as by day.

A far from gaudy plumaged bird, the nightingale sports a creamish grey front and underparts. The upper parts are warm brown and the plumage carries a texture of well-preened smoothness. The tail in dull weather appears russet, but in sunlight displays flares of red. The tail is balanced, narrow and rounded at the end.

If disturbed the bird ceases singing and dives swiftly into cover. The experts tell us that this species, perhaps not surprisingly, nests in deep herbage and close to the ground. The nest is well cupped, I seem to remember reading on the back of a boyhood cigarette card, the four or five eggs being blotched or flecked with red. The young are fledged and skulking in the underbush at nearly a month old, perhaps before that time. How soon the male youngsters develop the buzzes, trills, flute notes and whistles that makes them so popular when heard within the bird watching fraternity is difficult to define. Possibly in the summer a year after they have hatched. And I would think *definitely* the summer following.

In the journal of BMC Evolutionary Biology, author Conny Bartsch, having studied birdsong while researching for the Free University of Berlin, put forward the possibility of a bird's repertoire, if varied and lengthy, aiding the female in mate selection with regard to the singer's paternity values. If, for instance, the singing male attempts to impress and thereby attract a healthy and attractive mate, he may well prove to be an attentive parent and bring in more insect food for the young to feed on. He displays his 'potentially good mate' qualities in his song, *his singing.*

In nightingales, stresses Conny Bartsch, the mixture of song notes and specific variations – these important features of breeding development – are particularly noticeable. With all this in mind as I viewed the nightingale through Stuart's 'scope I decided that the cock bird perched out in the open and singing before us must surely fall into the category of 'good potential' mate. And, what is more, he was not afraid of humans dismantling their equipment at 20 or so feet.

Yet he appeared no more concerned than do yellow wagtails and starlings when they are closing in on the hoofed feet of grazing cattle which unwittingly force insects out from the grass blades and into the open, which is where the birds pick them off.

Besides this nightingale we heard, as we moved off, a nightingale rival, a willow warbler and blackcap bubbling and twining from the nesting thickets at the same time.

This year there is an estimated 30 pairs of nightingale nesting at Little Paxton.

A garden warbler put in a brief appearance. A palish bird, brownish grey about the nape, upper body, wings and tail and buffish white below. There would be a nest nearby, we decided, and in the time it took to make that decision this skulking, quiet little bird made off.

Out on the open water a pair of Canada geese shepherded a creche of *43* goslings of varied, but early hatched, sizes. I have long been aware of the fact that crèches within this species are not uncommon. But I have never seen so large a crèche surrounding or following just one goose and gander.

Sudden small flare of blueish green and scarlet skimming above the water surface in direct flight. Kingfisher!

Such a varied selection will do fine for one day. Thank you, Little Paxton.

# MAY

## Cairngorm Plateau, Scotland

Stepping off the ski lift to follow the outline of Pat walking several yards ahead of me and beyond whom looms an enveloping mist as our walking boots seek purchase within the shelvings of stones and slabs of granite.

The Cairngorms. At last! The stoniest place in Europe! The schoolboy who first saw photographs and read of them while perusing bookshops on Saturday mornings arises jubilant within my mind. *You're there! You're here, walking across a plateau that you first saw in photographs. It's taken all of 50 years, son, but you've made it.*

Unfamiliar terrain. Not a twig, leaf or blade of grass in sight. A lunar landscape. Our spacecraft is back there by the ski lift hut, or so it feels.

There is a slight sense of clambering as we collectively file along this section of the plateau. And with the hard, metallic smells of winter infiltrating the nostrils. Blazes of snow on opposite rock terrains penetrate the mist veil. Inhospitable? To the minds of many people, yes, but this plateau has its champions, not the least of whom was Nan Shepherd who wrote *The Living Mountain* during the Second World War. The manuscript remained in a drawer for thirty or so years and was first published in 1977. Read Nan Shepherd and you have this massif – its life, atmosphere and weathers – in the extending grasp of your outdoor literary hand. Nor does she strive to make the place a shrine of goodness and meditation. On the contrary she mentions its tragedies – the people who perished while climbing or wandering there – within the first few pages.

The Plateau was Nan Shepherd's most extensive exploration of the Cairngorm Mountain Range. Or so I gathered from first reading *The Living Mountain*. From her prose I learned that the massif is made up of granite which rises to 4,000 feet, and I gained the impression that there are summits of around the same height that are known by every Cairngorm enthusiast.

From most of the Plateau that I walked the often unspectacular mountainscapes are spread below. There is no gazing upwards in awe. Nevertheless, it is a different place; a huge rock trap swathed in mist and, on the days I visited, under cloud.

Snow blanketing summits and weather exposed is really the only natural element that, because of its contrast, holds the eye for a time.

Not only Nan Shepherd but a great many people, past and in the present, know The Cairngorms as the average person knows his or her living room. But it is the contrasts – the further explorations and weather changes, some of which can be quite severe – that provide each stalwart climber or walker with explorations so challenging and memorable.

My first starry saxifrage flora I was shown up there. Flurries of moss campion taking advantage of the seemingly tiny fissures hewn by evolution and land movement into the walls of pink granite. I am surprised to see natural 'posies' of eyebright here and clumps of milk vetch, both of which have to be named for me because this is my first experience of being in a region of mountain flora. Nan Shepherd emphasises in her work how these plants flourish close to the ground and generally out of the wind's icy blast. Evolution ensuring that all is well within the great mysterious jigsaw again; keeping its great house spotless with nothing out of place.

The first brace of ptarmigan startle me and, yes, they are still in white winter plumage. Their proximity I find intriguing as they accept our group, pausing now to observe them, the birds almost as close in as foraging city pigeons. When a brace take off we hear the 'whirr' of air and wings as is the case with most rotund-shaped game birds. They do not, however, fly far. And seldom completely out of sight. In all probability the flights have little to do with human proximity, or so I believe. And, like most sudden short flights that birds as pairs undertake, they are probably ignited by the pair bonding will of the female.

When ptarmigan pairs settle on or around boulders of granite they attempt to play female-hide-and-male-seek but briefly. They then re-emerge out in the open and stand regarding us passing humans as partridges do cattle.

Mountain zone bird experts state that the female ptarmigan undergoes three plumage changes a year and the male four. Their bonding calls I can only interpret as sounding like 'urrr-uur', which, if they call when flying, doubles their wing whirring presence.

Their feet are downy but the foreclaws are prominent and needed to aid the birds when they are scrambling over gravelly slopes and boulders. To the human eye, usually confined to accessible mountain tracks, the food of the ptarmigan seems to be in relatively short supply; sparse. But, of course, they venture over rocky terrain seldom seen by Cairngorm visitors, let alone walked.

Shoots, budding leaves of mountain flora and berries are the basics of their diet, but the mountains must yield insects because a ski lift operator assures me that ptarmigan also feed on insects and feed their chicks *only* on insects.

If, then, there are long spells of summer rain the chicks are likely to perish, which is probably why there is not a *surfeit* of these inquisitive birds in any known region of The Cairngorms.

Here, too, I first sight dotterel – attractive members of the plover family – which, from The Cairngorms, migrate and return to breed probably in the same regions as where they were hatched. Like the ptarmigan, these swollen-bellied, leggy, but equally proportionate, birds appear to be unafraid of humans. The breeding dress of the male – the buffs, browns, orange or russet breast tones with white slicings about the head – is distinctive to say the least. They favour dry mountain-type heath and, on passage during the winter, endless tracts of European steppe-type country.

Again, I am surprised on discovering that dotterel are basically insect feeders, which, of course, includes larvae. There has to be, therefore, sufficient food supplies for both ptarmigan and dotterel in this terrain, otherwise the birds would not be here.

Wedged into a terrain of rock, I break for 'elevenses', comprising of flapjack, with wandering veteran Thiery de Paun. He and I share a spiritual awareness of cloud, varied terrain and light creating an ever-changing effect in accordance with the time of day and seasonal tapestry.

At a Boat-o-Garton guest house I explained the nature of my work in classrooms, in woodlands or by rivers teaching environmental themes, then Thiery told me of his days – again spent out of doors – working the boats and barges of the Belgium water authorities collecting water samples throughout the region.

A family man, it takes Thiery three days to travel from Belgium to The Cairngorms and, of course, three days to return. His hungering for the heights he calls his 'annual migration'. Had we been born with mountains on our respective doorsteps, instead of flatlands and water, we agree that we might well have become mountaineers, or at least high country rambling guides.

Away from The Cairngorms massifs Thiery and I – scanning Lock Varr through binoculars – marvel at the noonday light enhancing the exquisite feather-sheened splendour and red eyes of the pair of Slavonian grebe nesting on a partly submerged branch disfiguring the shoreline; are intrigued by the crested tit, my first, flittering through the low herbage of an Abernethy Forest glade, insects pincered in its bill with which to feed its young; and watch the behavioural modes of the King Eider drake aware of us and putting the eider ducks and their darkly clustering broods of ducklings between we birdfolk and himself at Newburg Bay near Aberdeen. This particular King Eider is a local regular far from the high Arctic where he probably pipped an eggshell and wintered along the coastlines of northern Norway or in Iceland.

Who knows? This individual may have been clipped or injured by gunshot. Nevertheless, he has adapted well within the eider assembly here at Newburg. Thiery, incidentally, has seen him on every one of his annual visits. An adult by now, of course, the King Eider sports a brownish orange bill and orange frontal shield. The cheeks are splashed in pale grey on a contrasting gunmetal tone. A black and white slender line separates the cheeks from the pale blueish neck, nape and headtop. This line rises to form an irregular-type apex above the drake's marble black eye. The crop is pinkish buff, the back a varying sheen of strong flight feathers, and above the feet and edging up to the stern is a white patch. Peculiar but colourful and, therefore, conspicuous is the King Eider.

This individual sports with the ducks of the eider breed (*Somateria mollissima*) of which there are many in breeding rafts riding the wind-driven waves. The drakes of these northern coastline eider are black and white, conspicuous and tolerant of the King Eider's presence.

Mid-morning in the Findhorn Valley, the necklacing water to our left, a rough track ahead and a striving summit clothed in heather blocking out an even sense of horizon and levelling, as the track demands, with our left shoulders. We humans remark on the splendour of the heather and are cut off from the terrain. Not so the three golden eagles quartering the heathery summit. Raptors. The name serves them well. A powerful, tantalising image quartering in low-level flight, and those steady wing strokes creating thermals should the hook-billed birds not find thermals for themselves.

Even in silhouette, the elasticity and primary suppleness of those wings magnetise the seasonal eye due to the seemingly effortless pattern of flight.

Thiery and I learned from the eagle-watching regulars here that the Findhorn Valley plays host to relatively young birds. Singletons which come together after being driven from their natal range by their parents once they can hunt for themselves. Why this should be no one can say, but most immature birds have assembly points and flocking grounds where they feed, meet and, some, pair off.

Through binoculars, Thiery and I look for the white wing patches which are definable on two but the third appears darker, plumage-wise, in the lower body and may prove to be an adult. Unmated perhaps. Or an adult in its first year of adulthood.

This trio rise and lower, glide and soar. Flight-wise they want for little and are, therefore, the masters of the nearby crags. The adult-type circles, drops, circles again, then swoops. For seconds it is on the ground and its head, scrutinising something below it, is all that can be seen. And even then the raptor is looking round, checking all four sides.

It rises. In its talons the eagle holds a sizeable body. I would think its prey to be too big for a mountain hare. More like a newly-born red deer calf or a *stillborn* one. There is no struggle. The golden eagle's prey remains prone and seemingly curled. There are no slender legs dangling. Could it even be a vixen? Difficult to say, especially as the raptor flies away from us and into the blinding light. A memorable encounter, Thiery and I agree.

Later we are back at the flapjack, sitting on what appears to be a natural cairn. The next day we are flapjacking again and I'm gazing at rocks and sky until Thiery taps me and exclaims, "Look!" He points to a stand of larch perhaps a quarter of a mile away but which are being unevenly segregated by an elongated swathe of white as a steam train cuts swiftly along the line alongside them. Something not seen every day. And Thiery is as delighted as I, even though mankind has played out his role in the creation of that engine, which knows nothing of life let alone the changing seasons.

Abernethy Forest – pines and silver birches of the old Caledonian range. Here, Land Rover ensconced, we travel a track and see a splendid roebuck nibbling herbage. It has its pale rump to us, and its strangely forked antlers are still encased in protective 'velvet', which will be shed as the warmer weeks progress.

The roebuck swings its head over its rump to stare at the Land Rover, its silky jaws moving to position the strands of herbage it has plucked from a fruiting thicket.

I'm expecting the roebuck to bound off into the forest as those I have seen, singletons usually, skimming soundlessly through glades lit by the low evening light of the early Highland summer. To my amazement the roebuck, other than continue staring with only its jaws rotating, remains within 10 feet of us. The eyes are alert, the muzzle black and, to the human touch, probably moist as that of a domestic dog.

The shoulders are well set to hold the antlers of a rival should the buck meet with a rival in the incoming rutting season. The back is long, chestnut brown in pelage texture and the tail paler and contrasting with the slimly boned, yet powerful, flanks.

As long as the Land Rover continues on its way and we humans remain within it, so the buck remains. I have known park-bred red deer stags display more natural caution.

Capercaillie! Listen to that whirring call. The hen bird is on eggs in nearby underbush; the displaying cock, stepping defensively over our intended path in the already bruised grasses and fronds, is surely slightly larger than a farmyard goose, darkly feathered – blacks, hints of brown, dark grey. The head is uplifted and the ruff of chin feathers extended. His wings are lowered and the primaries trailing on the ground like those of a displaying mute swan. The tail is outfanned, every feather preened and in place. Immaculate, in fact.

Hissing and bubbling, the protective male intends to route us if we linger. The eye burns with avian intensity, the encircling eye patch is waxen red. Should we see a capercaillie in flight, Thiery explains, the tail, held well back, is dark brown in colour.

Should we not move at a pace accepted by the capercaillie cock, he will increase his pace while clicking his bill – the upper and lower mandibles – although the sound could be made from the throat, and bear down on us crop first.

The taste of capercaillie flesh, I decide, must surely render unpalatable to the average gourmet of game meat because the bird's chief food is pine needles, which are acidic or why wouldn't we eat them ourselves?

Although I have watched black grouse at the 'display, courtship and deciding grounds' known as a 'lek', on the Staffordshire moorlands, I have not met anyone who has watched capercaillie, although there will be enthusiasts living on the edges of Abernethy and The Cairngorms who have filmed the spectacle, and understandably.

Beside pine needles, capercaillie show a digestive preference to aspen leaves and berries. Grit to aid in the digestion of this unusual combination is taken from the earth and the fringes of the forest rides.

We doubt that the hen bird will rise from the eggs if we pass close to the nest. Nor are we intending to antagonise the cock bird any further. We withdraw, sideways. He steps on, bubbling, gobbling, beak clicking. Not too far out from where he knows the hen to be prone and defensive over the egg clutch, he halts. We are over his boundary line, off his territory. Those few glades of that Abernethy stretch back there are his alone.

Looking at a map of The Cairngorm Plateau, Thiery and I admit that so much occupied our eyes and minds that we were never aware whether or not we were scouting Ben Macdui, Beinn Bhrotain or Braeraich, and by 'scouting' I mean the lower slopes. What we did, however, is keep moving. Keep looking and seeing. The flapjack snacks aside, we had no time for lounging. Nor did we intend there to be time.

Come the winter, I shall settle in an armchair with *The Living Mountain* by Nan Shepherd taking me back to those heights but through the eyes of a fully experienced seasonal stalwart.

And my own Cairngorm experiences? I will never forget them.

It was at the ages of around ten or eleven that I first set eyes upon the topographical area known as The Cairngorm Range or, by some mountaineering writers, simply The Cairngorms. Nor was I looking at a destinations chart on the platform of the city railway station. Instead I was in one or other of the five large bookshops that my natal city could rightfully boast of. In the heart of that city, yes, and usually on a Saturday morning.

In one bookshop that became my regular, a book caught my eye because a man on the cover photograph appeared to be clinging – and therefore dependable on his hands, knees, feet and survival ingenuity – to a rock face.

That was my first experience of seeing someone seemingly fastened by his own sheer skills to a deadly natural wall, which, rope aided, he intended, one way or another, to breach. Rock climbing, mountaineering? I had never heard of the terms.

The book's title was *Mountaineering in Scotland*. Its author was W H Murray. Murray's image was almost superseded by that of the bookshop's overseer, a tall woman – probably ex-Forces – who came and stood, hands behind her back, beside me each time I browsed the books in that particular shop. What she could only have seen was me with clean hands turning the book's pages with respect, including those bearing photographs. As I'm sure I have written elsewhere, the woman stood her ground and I stood mine. Adults could browse books. And so obviously could ten-year-old boys who, it seemed, so far as society was concerned, were fit for little until they were 18 when they were packed off to a war zone and awarded a place in a dugout trench where they were expected to fire rounds of ammunition at innocent 18-year-olds in another trench and were referred to as 'the enemy'. *That was all right*. But educate ourselves and exercise our curiosities before that time was not expected of us.

However, overshadowing the bookshop overseer were the names and literary associations of the authors whose books I chose to browse. And the most prominent was W H Murray, whose name I would see and articles I would read in most of the outdoor magazines of my then future.

Needless to say I never became a mountaineer, largely I suppose because I was too busy walking canal and river towpaths, exploring old farms and outbuildings, roaming over moors and through woods, while seeking out loners such as myself. Consequently, the only time I touched upon W H Murray was when I read his work, including his exploits while taking part in world-renowned expeditions.

In 1941, when I was aged four, Murray, born in Liverpool in 1913, was called up for military service after registering a year earlier. As a 2nd Lieutenant in 1942, he was posted to Iraq, Cyprus and twice to North Africa where he took part in The Western Desert Campaign in which he served as a Captain.

He left the Army in 1946 and I, as a RAF conscript, arrived in his Northern African footsteps, or close on I liked to think, a decade later.

Although W H Murray wrote some eighteen to twenty mountaineering books, his remarkable achievements – and those of close companions like Tom Weir and Douglas Scott – were never to be assigned to the national archives and completely forgotten.

Recognising challenge and endurance, both present and past, Robin Lloyd-Jones wrote *The Sunlit Summit – the life of W H Murray* and it was published by Sandstone Press Ltd in 2013. That same year the work was awarded as a Saltire Society Research Book and deservedly so. The book is a literary memorial to the doyen of all outdoor folk serving out his life as he rightly thought fit both before and after the Second World War.

The book's Appendix 1, obviously so admirably researched – again by Robin Lloyd-Jones – includes national and world changes in Murray's time and, as yet, is the most comprehensive I have studied. And, fittingly, the last entry records Murray's death in hospital, possibly due to heart surgery complications, on 19 March 1996, aged 83 years.

Following his nationally known expeditions and achievements, Murray's sidekick, Tom Weir, continued rambling and writing largely for *The Scotsman* magazine in which I read his essays every month.

Towards the end of his life Weir appeared in several television features based, of course, on Scotland, and the great outdoors. It was in these programmes that Weir came over as a roistering entertainer as well as the genial outdoor man that those of us similarly affected would have been delighted to have met.

Another mountaineer, whose book *Survival Count* intrigued me, was Gwen Moffat. She was a mountain face/sheer wall expert who wrote economically about her achievements and the people who enrolled as her guide-seeking students. And I soon gathered that she made a dual living as a writer and climber of renown, and who regularly conducted her day – or longer – courses on mountaineering and outdoor survival skills summer or winter alike.

It requires pluck to take on a relatively inexperienced protégé and have them roped to you without, in the first stages, really knowing of their capabilities. But Gwen Moffat had that pluck and her accounts, however brief because she was not by any stretch of the imagination a 'flowery writer', held me to her pages. Moreover I read Moffat several times just as I did W H Murray. Am I a suppressed mountaineer? Sometimes I wonder.

In her advanced years Moffat took to writing fictional who-dun-its, I believe, and retired to a cottage in, or close to, the Yorkshire National Park. And, although I never met the lady, I was always of the opinion that she was very much her own person, as are most outdoor people.

What it means to be a mountaineer really came home to me when I was in the carriage of a Cairngorm-bound train pulling in at the steep inclined settlement of Dalwinnie, one Saturday midday. Onto the platform alighted a single passenger. A man of early middle age, tall, powerfully built and draped in mountaineering equipment, including crampons. Only a sledge and husky team were missing.

Ignoring his immediate surroundings, the mountaineer stared at the great rock mass of heights as if in silent worship. In the hours and days that followed for me his image, *his allegiance* to that particular tract of high Scotland, recurred to the point of me having to take up a pen and pad and attempt a poem, if only to exorcise that image. Thus came:

## ALIGHTING AT DALWINNIE

*One kindred spirit, sleek dark hair, in his thirties,*
*looks westward above and beyond the stationary train*
*to the snow capping the crowns of bronze brown rock.*

*Bereft of a microphone, his facial expression conveys*
*his relief at seeing them there as if he*
*suspected they had been re-sited overnight,*
*or his past visits, he recently discovered,*
*were nothing more than ascents effortlessly traversed in*
*dreams.*

*To The Cairgorms he has returned and is*
*about to report to his psychic. Convince himself that*
*he is off the train. Free of home, office and a*
*salary-imprisoning five-day week partially*
*spent obeying the demands of a computer screen.*

*Some city to the south,*
*perhaps Edinburgh, London, caves away from*
*his shoulders when his eyes settle*
*on the wealth amongst which he will*
*regain his true character.*

*Rucksack and crampons his well-chosen companions,*
*he stands as the guard blows his whistle,*
*the train lurches northwards. Lone figure,*
*city drained, turned as if sculptured in marble*
*towards those year-long beckoning peaks.*

*Dalwinnie. Thirty years ago I was told by a*
*long-distance lorry driver of the red deer that*
*hunger and blizzard winds herd down to the roadside,*
*thrust their muzzles up to the cabs of parked lorries.*
*Feed ravenously on proffered crusts and cheese.*

*Come the summer, like the climbers, the deer will make*
*for the tops. But today's lone mountaineer will*
*descend reluctantly but months ahead of them.*
*He will not be around to experience*
*the winter when it comes.*

## Loch Garton, Speyside

From the hide and through powerful binoculars, I view the female osprey standing centralised in the nest hollow of the nationally famous pine. Descending from his spectacular display flight, the male flies in, hovering briefly to gain descending momentum, his tail outspread, wing tips quivering, before he lifts the wings entirely and, with toes outspread, settles onto the twiggy high-branched island of the nest.

The recently built platform holds both ospreys. For seconds they stand together. Out there they may be uttering low courtship tones, some form of avian speech.

The female lowers her wings from the back, thereby enticing the male to mount her. He responds, again after seconds, and, with wings open and circling to give him balance coordination, connects accordingly. One act of coition takes ten to fifteen seconds, the female remaining statuesque, the male pressing downward and inward with wings windmilling.

With coition over, the male steps from the female's back, turns sideways to her, then springs forward to ride and ascend the sky, forest and lochscapes above and around the nest. The female remains, preens, tidies the ruffled feathers of her back.

As every member of the Royal Society for the Protection of Birds is aware Loch Garten's original osprey pair were the unwitting avian characters of an unyielding success story. A pair arriving to nest here in the mid-1950s were the first to adopt Britain as a breeding base for 50 years. The species had been persecuted by gamekeepers and egg collectors to the point of localised extinction.

As every young naturalist knows, the Loch Garten ospreys were indeed the forerunners of a tremendous success story; aided somewhat by human agency, but a success story nevertheless.

Eminent field naturalists and birdwatchers made annual trips, and the then editor of *Shooting Times and Country* magazine Philip Brown wrote the book *The Ospreys of Loch Garten*, which tied in with the *Survival* TV series produced by Colin Wilcock.

Brown's account gave a fascinating insight into both osprey behaviour and the first efforts to warden the nest and site, particularly during the nights. Viewing the ospreys entailed entering the sanctuary which was quickly established by the Royal Society for the Protection of Birds.

The ospreys were watched, and are still, from a hide, through a telescope and at a respectable distance.

Usually before a female osprey arrives at a site, the male has arrived ahead of her and has already established a territorial breeding zone over which he performs spectacular flights and continues to do so when the female settles in. An estimated 1,000 feet are covered in the male's ascent at his chosen highest point, at which he briefly hovers then swoops downwards – either to the waters of a loch, a forest perch or the eyrie which a female will likely as not be occupying.

When hunting, the flight of the osprey describes a flapping pattern and appears slow. But the predator is using its eyes, especially when above water.

By now many bird and wildlife enthusiasts, if they have not witnessed the osprey diving for themselves, will have seen television footage of an osprey descending and securing a fish, usually a pike or trout. The osprey plunges, there appears in some instances a brief submergence, then the wings appear tent-like above the water surface and, in a sudden swish of spray, the osprey rises with a fish in its talons. This 'fish hawk' feeds on nothing *but* fish, I hasten to add, and its preference for trout aided in the extermination of the species. The trout enthusiasts and gamekeepers declared war collectively.

In 1968, five osprey chicks were reared in the Loch Garten region and more pairs are now nesting in Scotland, but with the Loch Garten pair used as the honey trap residents in a successful bid to entice human visitors to one spot and allow other osprey pairs in less-known – perhaps more remote – regions to prosper with only the minimal wardening taking place to ensure that 'outsider' breeding pairs survive and rear, where possible, an annual brood.

In October the ospreys journey south, mainly to southern Asia or the tropics of Africa. Infrequently, those on their autumn passage flights can be seen around the large and relatively remote reservoirs of England as en route to the warmer climes. They pause for a brief time to fulfil their hunger. They may stay an hour or a day. Usually one bird, or a pair, to a region. But they do not remain.

## A9 En Route For Inverness

In a roadside café I'm introduced by Thiery to a mountaineer who prefers to remain nameless 'if you're going to write about it'.

Weathered with life-experience lines lightly creasing his cheeks, despite the faint beard, the mountaineer endorses Thiery's telling of a corrie which remains snow blocked and almost unyielding throughout each year. He points out the locations on the map in Nan Shepherd's *The Living Mountain*, a copy of which I have stowed into my rucksack.

Wedged into the hip line of Braeraich, Scotland's third highest mountain, is Garbh Choire Mor but which, when translated, furnishes mountaineers with the mind picture of a most inhospitable place in the name of Big Rough Corrie. The snow seldom leaves this corrie, which experts claim has retained snow certainly since the late sixteenth and early seventeenth centuries when records were probably begun.

The snow has thawed five times since 1700 and these were in the last and present centuries, the last noticeable thaw having taken place in 2006. Whether these recent thaws occurred as a result of climate change is not fully known. Along with the mountaineer and Thiery I have my doubts. However, for the most part, the terrain is regarded as one huge snowdrift trapped in and by time. At the most, the mountaineer explains, there could be 70 feet or more of snow trapped and frozen there still. It is a glacial valley shaped by ice movement and held in a quasi-solidified state since the great Ice Age departure of 140,000 years ago when the caves of Cresswell Crags in my natal Nottinghamshire lured in the Nomadic human tribes, following, in their generations, the receding ice.

Six or seven of the snow swathings are known as 'snowfields' and, as early as October, the blizzards come sweeping in on temperatures below zero and can lead to 10 to 12 feet drifts. The corrie is obviously positioned to catch and hold the snow which, by the Christmas of most years, is the only definite natural element within the entire terrain.

There are, the mountaineer further informs us, incredible tunnels and bridges formed from congealed snow and ice up there. And, yes, he has explored them.

I was equally surprised to learn that the Ben Nevis range has also nurtured snowfields since the last weeks of 2006. Another pause in the forking of the haggis I was tackling.

# JUNE

## Coombes Valley RSPB Reserve, Staffordshire

Leaving the bird hide where the antics of a male great spotted woodpecker has delighted us in his varied *and successful* attempts to extract food morsels from the bird feeder, a nudge and a pointing finger are all that are needed to direct your attention to the red-pelted dog stoat exploring the inner tunnel of a partially ruined drystone wall. Many stones are bereft on the wall's nearest side thus allowing the stoat to enter without difficulty and explore, with whiskers measuring the space on either side and twitching, the tunnel, at the end of which could well be a nest of wheatear, spotted flycatcher or pied wagtail chicks. These it will remove from the nest at its leisure one by one and possibly feed to its own kits. There may be a nest filled with fledglings or, after the stoat's past predations, there may be one remaining.

I love the rippling movement of its stalking body. The sheen of its red pelage, small but elongated due to the stoat's shape, rippling according to the plays of light and shade.

It is not for us to intervene. The themes of wild nature must take their varied routes according to the lore of survival. And, in any case, I doubt this will be the only drystone wall tunnel which the stoat will be exploring. It has probably several fledgling larders established throughout its hunting range.

I see that you have listed already the singing cock birds hereabout: the lesser white throat by the car park hedgerow; the several willow warblers in the budding hawthorn scrub on either end of the track that we've walked down.

Willow warbler singing on the top of the hawthorn tree, look! And a dipper poised but characteristically 'dipping' on one of the many green mossed rocks segregating the channels of the silvering Coombes Brook. Couple of male grey wagtails hereabout too. Territorial rivals and intent on seizing mayfly or damselfly which – silvered and barely ethereal wisps – make up the proportions of a meal for a bird or its fledglings.

Back to the wall because the stoat has abandoned it and is racing along its top but too fast for me to tell whether or not it had prey clenched in its jaws.

At the same time that we glimpse pied flycatchers in the hawthorns on this near slope, a hen sparrowhawk wings over. She flies direct and is not currently hunting but, again, could be carrying prey to feed a brood.

The steps which the wardens have woven into the steep ridgeside here are welcome because they take us within satisfying viewing range of the nest boxes put up for the pied flycatchers. As that ever-pioneering naturalist, the late Bill Condry, discovered, pied flycatchers rapidly adapt to nest boxes, particularly if they are sited in birch and oak woodlands situated in the west and north of Great Britain.

The cock birds carry white crops and alula wing patches. The tip of the forehead is white and the rest of the plumage black. The female is buffish brown where the male is black. They are stout little birds which carry small bills, and are reckoned to number around 20,000 throughout the British Isles. That is, I should add, during the breeding season which extends from May until the end of June. Hereabout for those of us involved in today's bird watching jaunt there is so much to see for the tree canopies serve today, and every summer day, as an avian city working the arterial branchways in the mute but overall search for food.

A tree pipit perched high and singing; wood warblers flicking through the leaf canopies; pair of nuthatches visiting a bird feeder. In a background tree canopy a jay perched watching a male great tit pirouetting and sideways hopping excitedly.

This scene I read as the great tit – intending to visit its nesting hole to feed its young – being aware that the jay was watching, as all members of the crow family do. When the great tit was away – collecting more food – the jay would perch at the entrance to the nest hole inside of which the chicks, aware that a shadow had appeared at the hole which meant food, would reach up and out to take it and be grabbed swiftly in the jay's bill to be dragged out and, in turn, serve as a meal. Visiting *Corvidae* at nesting holes can decimate an entire family of young birds in this way.

For the birdwatcher the bell-like calls of cock redstarts, to which a single female seems to be responding although she may be just out food prospecting; a binocular zoom-in of a lesser white throat singing, its grey cap rising and lowering as, turning its head, it attempts to sing in every direction, its rufous wings smart and eloquent in the patches of sunlight. And the birdwatcher lists grow: great tits singing and sub-singing; the pied flycatchers changing perches for singing with willow warblers; a hen sparrowhawk, the sex estimated by her wingspan, passing directly over the valley and so she too is flying directly to feed food to chicks; a dipper glimpsed with a caddis fly in its bills; the calls of the dipper chicks in their nest crevice hole competing with the sound of water gushing down its eon-old channels.

We, and the bird watching group, move on a few miles to:

## Swallowmoss

I first came across this lovely name in one of the first edition C F Tunnicliffe books which my mother bought me in the early 1950s. My first visit in winter coincided with the sunlight-silvered back and wingspan of a short-eared owl prospecting the heather harvest.

Today, as we walk the main side track, the bubbling calls of black grouse intercept the low twining concertos of cock whinchat perched on an upright stave supporting the drystone wall. One of the stavetop perchers proves to be female. Most, as we disturb them singularly, flit down and across our path to the biscuit-coloured tussocks on our right. There will be nests here, be assured of that, and the moss itself – thronged with young silver birch striking up between the heather masses – serves to aid both male and female wheatears perched on sprigs or courting in flickering flight – swift and weaving as butterflies – before diving together into the tussocks. Obviously there is a nest here because neither reappear.

In the walled field behind the barn three cock black grouse feed well apart, their lyre-shaped tails lowered under these food-seeking circumstances. But on the drystone wall across the far side of the field one is perched in display. He could well be the dominant bird of that particular patch or 'lekking' ground where, in previous weeks, he has made his presence known to his rivals. The dark blue neck sheen on this occasion is emphasised by the sunlight; the red wattle burns like an ember. Through powerful binoculars his eye appears glassy. Most of his wing plumage is blackish with a white wing bar and white undertail.

Glassing the fieldgrasses below his throne, we identify a curlew standing on a mound. If it is a cock bird he too may be attempting to define the borderlines of his chosen territory.

A whinchat through the lens is truly a shape that appeals instantly to the combinations of retina and cortex. We are talking about a combination comprising head, wings, tail and inners; rotund, *almost round*, in shape and about five inches of life wrapped up within that combination.

The crown of the male is streaked with black, the upper parts brown and, again, streaked with moorland shadow black – almost a camouflage. A swathing of orange cream – but pale orange rather than vivid – endows the crop or breast and belly.

The one we have in view today perches on a stem striking out at an angle of around 45 degrees. But, like all small birds, so long as it can lock its tiny toes around its perch and remain upright all is well with our subject. One whinchat perches on the looped handle of a farm gate. Perhaps a favoured perch in the short time it will be remaining here to see a possible two broods out of the nest.

Those whinchat and wheatears which perch on the highest silver birch bents or heather sprigs are obviously targets for raptors passing over, a raptor seeing and picking out one of the little birds at intervals throughout each day – the shape, not the colour, defining it as worthy prey – for beneath the body are the very ingredients the raptor is searching: the two tiny pumping breasts, holding the heart in place, along with the incredibly small gizzard and other innards. Having struck, the raptor – a merlin hereabout perhaps – will clench its shrieking victim, until there is no sound emitting from the voicebox, while flying to a tree or section of stone walling. Death administered on the wing, or close to it.

At the plucking block the merlin will tear tiny feather layers from the small heaving breast that is living beyond the main body of the victim itself, and cleave its short, hooked bill into the inners while grasping at and swallowing sinews. With its bill soon bloody and dripping, the raptor will at intervals raise its head – the challenging glare rendering it as a force of certainty. Thus yet another small bird succumbs before sunset.

Curlew call and the whinchat population go about their business undeterred.

Here, look! Sweeping low over the heather a male merlin mobbing a male kestrel. Those leafless trees – dead now but standing – must provide prey reconnaissance posts for them both. The flight manoeuvres between these two are masterful. There's much swooping and feigning and rounding in on each other. But neither will extend a leg to produce the clawed foot that may damage and gain first clench of the would-be opponent.

Probably while the nesting season is with us they meet like this, since both prey on small birds and mammals. But it's the merlin which catches the eye because he is our expert darter and looper, used and designed for catching swallows initially. The sparrowhawk, by comparison, is the aerial tornado. Rushing in and snatching at great, silent winged speed. Some of the birds on the birdwatcher's list may be taken by one or other of these predators in the days to come. Perhaps even in the *hours* or *minutes* to come. Who can say?

As for now, they loop and circle around each other over the heather tufts in the manner of bonding butterflies. They are making for what to us humans is a horizon. And there we must leave them. I doubt they will ever clash in combat but, as for aerial manoeuvres and outputs of energy, they are superb having put on this silent show as a fitting finale to end our day.

## Sherwood Forest, Nottingham

An item in the national press provokes a question. Due to April's sunlight, record numbers of small tortoiseshell, brimstone and peacock butterflies are now being recorded in what is considered to be perfect butterfly weather. The report describes them as being 'on the surge'. My question is: are there enough food plants to a butterfly acre to sustain them?

Here, as far away from the English shorelines as one can possibly be, we enjoyed the vast numbers of clouded yellows which delighted our forest glades in the 1980s. Employed at the time as a Countryside Ranger, I saw them in their trios and quartets almost daily but never once took a sighting for granted.

Another item appears in the newspapers later in the week. Painted Lady butterflies allegedly 'in their millions' are making their way from North Africa to Britain, a route that I took myself several times when I was an RAF conscript in the 1950s. Painted Ladies begin the 1,500-mile journey in Morocco. Skyborne, they are high flyers and travel at an estimated 30mph. In 2009 an estimated *eleven million* settled in Scotland. Their most sought-after food is thistles, although they will explore other plants. But why, I ask myself, do these butterflies need to migrate? In our winter they bask in Morocco and Libya. In the summer their need to seek out those thistles brings them over here. But where and when did it all start? And how did those early pioneering Painted Ladies know where the thistles were to be found, or, vice versa, was North

Africa as far into the heated climes as they managed to travel? Obviously they were at one with the migrational spectrum. But when and how did it all begin?

## Cresswell Crags, Nottingham

Travelling those 40 miles north of here to Cresswell Crags on the Nottinghamshire-Derbyshire border, diversities seep into the floodgates of the mind.

Steadily climbing the Derbyshire foothill roads between Church Warsop and Welbeck, the twists and turns in the sylvan highways, with their helpful gradient and deer crossing signs, have me first wondering why there is not a direct linear route. Not that I find the road bends unpleasant. On the contrary I nurture the possibility of surprise when negotiating them: the variations in tree heights; the sunlit-backed secrecy of glades; the bracken fronds, each one an incredible living entity like the leaf sprays and the hidden tree roots themselves.

The bracken fronds are high and, doubtless, beneath them are paths made by fox, badger, stoat, grey squirrel, dunnock and wren. Through gaps pheasant-rearing pens home into the mind's awareness of diversities and endorse a sense of modern-day authority and land lease or ownership. Gamekeepers patrol; a gatelodge of considerable age mutely suggests that the road user keeps moving.

Were these winding, half-forgotten roads laid over tracks made by twelfth- to fourteenth-century man and used by fifteenth-century carriage or coach? And did those windings have to do with making diversions around then well-matured stands of oak, beech and black poplar? Did the survival-motivated people of 13,000 years ago create hunting routes between the forest and their Cresswell Crags vastness through the embryo stages of what was to become a deciduous wilderness? Had these people the brain capacities to lay marking stones and notch plants or strike indicator scratchings on rocks so that they would find their way back to that almost secretive limestone gorge well before nightfall? I believe so.

We are all motivated by the need to survive. But in this, the twenty-first century, how puny seem our needs alongside those of the meat- and skin-dependent dwellers of 13,000 years ago. Another diversity fires my awareness of bygone forest hovels and the pageantry created by Homo sapiens on horseback. History edging onto natural history.

Although Nottinghamshire born, not until I was aged around 33 did I touch a section of the stones that once represented the ground or trench structure of King John's Hunting Palace back down the road there at what is today fittingly called King's Clipstone.

As for a sense of pageantry, I nurtured a hint of it when I wandered the heath and forestry tracts around Haywood Oaks. I *felt* it. Felt a *something* which opened yet another channel of diversity when I researched the area for a previously published book *Exploring Nottinghamshire.*

Haywood Oaks? This is where King John had his knights assemble annually, or so the story goes, and where he watched them at the lists for they had to prove that they were still worthy of the monies he handed out to them.

So, again, we have Homo sapiens on horseback, some finely clothed and skilled at forms of weaponry that could not only despatch a sizeable hart or stag but also a Homo sapien rival. Should this not have been enough, I was once shown a skull with an arrowhead embedded in it. Whose skull and whose arrowhead we don't know. But what we *do know* is that Homo sapien treachery, hatred and greed was readily festering in the times of the longbow *for real.* Well beyond the centuries when such skulduggery was used for laying the foundations of stage plays and film scripts. And all the foregoing took place then as today at around 5 feet 5–10 inches of Homo sapien-measured tree-trunk height.

Way above that, in the yawning tree branches, woodland birds and their out-of-the-nest youngsters at this time of the year spent long daylight hours searching leaf sprays and tree bark for food, *then* just as they are today. Insects were searching for lesser insects and aphids, and birds – hundreds and thousands of birds throughout the British Isles – were, *and still are*, searching for both.

From the car, forest glades with foliage backlit by the summer light appear to our modern eyes and minds to be pleasant. For the eyes of bygone man, by contrast, if the glades failed to hold game – or at least spoor that could be followed and a quarry species *tracked down* – then the panic that could divert and become a fear of starvation would have been conceived, and quickly. Today's habitats are, to some extent, managed. Again, by Homo sapiens. Yet we delvers of modern times strive to see or imagine the tracts of countryside that are relatively left to nature.

En route and nearing Cresswell Crags we will wander in managed surroundings. But managed to interpret how these relatively *short-lived* Homo sapiens survived while striving to hold together cave quarters, food and warmth when it could be persuaded to favour them. These primitives – as such we think of them – knew of day, night, hunger, brief fulfilment, the means and guile needed for hunting and procreation, nurtured, one would assume, by sexual attraction. They knew, too, about death and dying. To some considerable extent they developed, became tool makers, wall artists. Did they carve and ochre stain out or roughly paint animal forms and caricatures when the weather was inclement and forced them to remain in shelter? A shelter that today we people of the twenty-first century call home.

To the cave dwellers of Cresswell the cave was indeed home, although one time-slipped Homo sapien community may have used the limestone gorge, with its glistening water and cavernous securities, as winter quarters, I was told on a previous visit.

A winter shelter or retreat? Feasible, yes, but those who could tell us for certain were moved on, *or off*, the great chessboard of evolution, as we people of the twenty-first century will be moved off when the mind of the restless world develops further.

The limestone gorge? The trip into the past? Both remain in good manageable hands in the dip of land as yet hidden by the café and interpretive centre here at Cresswell Crags.

'Dear Cresswell Crags Man,

Who among you was the first to tentatively set foot in this gorge? From where did you come? I doubt far. But the generations of your forebears experienced conditions that made them so dependant on furs, skins and any form of shaft, branch or stone that could be used for tool making. Not one of the elements, beyond that which the Native Americans call 'The Great Mystery', planted you there, standing upright and baying for flesh and blood.

You had first to find the gorge and, with your predator-wary Homo sapien peers, decide that it was safe. And that decision wouldn't take what, in this the twenty-first century, we call 'a day' – daylight sandwiched between two screens of darkness.

You, or one of your ancestors, had to arrive. And not alone. Therefore, what natural source provoked you into wandering here? Or setting out to explore? My guess is *water*. You followed the icy necklace through a variable terrain and had the sense to know that it was going somewhere.

Water also surely brought in the mammoths, hippopotamus groupings, the scavenging hyenas, and, in fresh sediment above the Ice Age layers, reinforced the growth of greenery – both before and after the *last* Ice Age.

God, how you needed to be fashioning those weapons for without them how could there be meat, skins, fur and protection? How many families to a cave dwelling could survive together? Yet there must have been shows of temperament altercations. Or did that will and need to survive – collective in every sense of the word – hold you together closely, regarding yourselves perhaps as a near-threatened species, especially when each night and each winter settled its chill across the gorge.

The caves must at times have reeked of blood, fat, flesh and the semen of each possible breeding being amongst you. Were there cases of rape, pillaging, murder? Disobedience separating the young from the elders? Theft, too, possibly? Of mate and possessions.

The pity is that you never became diarists. Yet creativity, *beyond* those themes embracing the need and will to survive, found you scratching out animal forms and daubing colours on cave walls.

There were those among you who saw beauty shaped by the form of an animal muscle, its flank, dewlap, neck, skull shape. You knew also that they could not be created by Homo sapiens but they could be recorded the next best way, in forms of art.

There are generations of secrets, of relics and artefacts yet to be uncovered in this seemingly settled community gorge to which you hastened when lightning ripped fire flares of unevenness across the sky, or blizzards obscured the tracks that you had previously made and were set to home by, and the demonic cry of the wind chilled you with the dread of possible isolation and loss of family, self and future existence.

How you communicated I would have found absorbing to say the least. You knew that you had voices because not only yourselves when young but your offspring used them, no doubt to good affect, when they were uncomfortable or afraid. Smiles, frowns, raging toothache and terminal disease you experienced yet with the quirk of admirable stubbornness that ensured you would be around the following day, month or year until it was your time to succumb as must we all.

I try to imagine a family man of your colony carving or painting the antlers of a stag while his children played with the knuckle and toe bones of the animals he had killed and the family eaten. His mate – woman – pondering over meat and herb storage; fashioning perhaps some kind of platter or utensil. If the summers were warm enough perhaps you all ate outside. But in the winter as far back inside the cave as relative warmth and comfort allowed.

I would imagine that the eyes of your people were relatively dark, the teeth of the elders, if they hadn't lost them, yellowing. The jaw settings in profile, some anthropoid in shape but bearded on the men.

The silence of time and distance will prevent you from replying. But, rest assured, you are not forgotten.'

At the entrance to Church Hole, probably inspiring the desire to create a record of the animals of his time and also perhaps because he could stand upright and light was available, a man – or so we imagine it to be – drew and etched. Not unlike myself, he revered the shapes of deer, allowed them to filter into the artistic galleries of his mind. The roe, the red deer and the elk. And, understandably, I wonder if at times he paused in his etching time to just marvel at the light yet, to our eyes, beautifully coordinated gait of these animals.

Did he recognise the fact that every set of antlers differs genetically in some small way? The antlers in the caves, taken from the beasts he had needed to slaughter –

did he know that the young stags or elk carried fewer tines and a narrower antler span than their older, dominant herd members?

Church Hole surrendered a needle made of bone to its modern archaeologists, along with what was probably the shin bone of a horse. There were notched artefacts.

And who gave the Robin Hood Cave its name? Long, long after the Cresswell cave dwellers there were forest outlaws and brigands supposed to have used it as a hide-out. If so, why not the other caves? But I think the legend creators of the Victorian age gave the cave that particular name.

In the Robin Hood Cave were found the many broken bones of Arctic hares. The bones carried cut marks which indicates how carefully those early Cresswell people removed both the skins for garment making and the meat for devouring.

An early archaeologist to Cresswell, back in the mid-1980s when I first visited as a Countryside Ranger, suggested that generations of these people developed the art of laying traps for these hares.

The same people probably valued the lower jaw and throat skins of the red deer and elk they killed long before the Normans credited these mammals with such warmth-creating luxuries, which was valued in the same way as the ermine coats of northern hemisphere stoats.

Again in the Robin Hood Cave a horse rib had been stained in ochre. Whether the artist worked on the head and forequarters when the horse was on the floor of the cave before him and ready to be butchered, or he worked from memory, who could say? But to my eyes it is a wonderful, yet obviously primitive, form of work. The horse of that time – we learn from this ochre discovery – was short muzzled compared to the horses of modern times but the artist, in this instance, had depicted the lower jawline, nostril and eye so neatly. Had he known of it, Queen Victoria's favourite artist, Edwin Landseer – who gained incredible likenesses in his works of dogs, deer and, to a lesser extent, horses – would have been equally impressed.

The rib carrying this drawing is polished but it doesn't have to come from Cresswell. It could have been carried there with much else by a Cresswell-bound ancestor following the water to the gorge, as I think of it. That said, there is a *good chance* of the work, for, yes, I regard it as such, having originated at Cresswell.

The Pin Hole Cave yielded amongst its findings a human-type figure. Again carved along the rib of a large mammal. Gods and goddesses? Was Cresswell Crags Man so far developed as to mentally create an entity to worship? I don't think anyone can be sure.

In the interpretive centre today are the skull of a hyena and a taxidermist's display model of a hyena, surprising due to its size. There is also a fragment of lion bone, the dead animal probably having been eaten by hyenas as the small information plaque suggests.

Returning south down the A614, we reached the traffic island where, for once in Nottingham, the land contours rise like a tidal wave frozen in time above the road. Being in the passenger seat I see again what my natal county has produced by way of a horizon. It isn't much but that horizon stands out simply because it has no rivalling horizons. At intervals three or four small trees, which distance prevents me from identifying, intercept the horizon and resemble lookouts posted to ensure that all is well.

As, in the car, we round the island, I can barely fail to notice that the north-westerly-facing slopes of the field are sown with a greening fieldcrop. What mastery of the tractor it must take to create furrows in so difficult-looking a terrain. Yet this field and its neighbours are never left unmanaged.

In the fieldcrop I notice a brown oval shape, like a scar burnt into the greenery. A hare in its form. Its chestnut eyes positioned at the side of the head must take in the traffic on the road below. What it makes of these objects we have no idea. Do hares become transfixed as seemingly do thousands of our own kind when watching television? I doubt it. The mammalian brain, or what little exists of its working parts, surely doesn't allow for that.

Mammals of the field work on instinct and glands. Therefore, the hare will never lose the feeling of vulnerability which surrounds it, even when it is resting and digesting food while in its form.

If we were to lean, binoculars in hand, on the fieldgate to survey the hare, we would see the long ears settled back along, or just flanking, its dorsal ridge, the varied tones of fawn or chestnut and small fleckings of black pebbledashing its pelage.

When the hare rises, those powerful hindquarters will convey it along one of its selected paths across the field.

A lone hare? Only in the first instance. There will be others similarly food seeking or in their forms within a hundred or two lopes of each other.

If it's a male, or 'jack', he will be aware of the forms used by his 'jill', his young 'jack' contenders for her attention, his out and out territorial rivals. Should it be a 'jill' she may be facing the direction her young, or 'leverets', are facing and possibly feeling the stirrings of yet more young life, as yet unborn, but thriving inside her. Her teats may be sore due to suckling; her underparts may smell of spilt milk or the best substance that she can produce as such.

But whether jack or jill, each hare in its form rests with whiskers occasionally quivering and almost indiscernible nostrils sucking in the scents of the fields and all that is at ground or hedgerow level around it. What they make of the distant traffic is one thing, but the fact that they are heel sprung and seldom taken by surprise, quite another. Those hares know more about what is happening in and around that north-westerly-facing field slope today than the Homo sapien who, within his modern society, owns it. Of that I have no doubt.

A friend, just returned from my beloved Dorset, surprises me with photographs he has taken of opium poppies. Apparently opium thrives splendidly in this south coastal chalk country. This is my first awareness of opium being grown legally in England. It is needed as a painkiller apparently – morphine to be used in hospitals – my equally surprised friend informed me after localised investigation.

I have also recently driven by mustard farms and in doing so recalled reading that mustard seed has been in use since the Romans arrived in Britain. As ingredients, the Romans also used vinegar – or its early days likeness – and ground almonds. Mustard as we know it was pioneered in 1814 by Jeremiah Colman, a Norwich businessman. Their mustard is made up of brown and white mustard seeds, sugar, spices, water and flour. The Americans, I understand, manufacture a milder mustard popular with the consumers of hot dogs.

## Nottingham

Way back in the 1970s I picked up a book on bees by the American naturalist Edwin Way Teale and became well and truly fascinated.

Had I the land I could well have become an apiarist. Since that time I have read several more books on the life of bees, going over old ground admittedly but with fascinating new insights coming into fruition with each decade and researchers' conclusions.

Watching the hives at a safe distance in the orchard of keen apiarist Bill, we discuss the world of these tiny pollen seekers, a singleton of which, at first sight, can create a sudden wariness in the boldest amongst us.

Bill and I remind ourselves of what we have read and were told back in our school days. We have nothing new to add since we are not researchers. Even less scientists.

The haze of bees that we observe around the hive through binoculars will be worker bees. In short, females.

The males have, or *are*, mated or mating with the queen, after which act their genitalia are torn off and having literally served their purpose in life they die. The *non-breeding* males are regarded as rejects and are forced to perish. They have nothing to offer the reproductive nectar-embroiled manufacturing system.

The nectar collected by the worker bees is processed by a dual process involving chemicals and physical involvement, and the enzymes convert the sugary substances while moistness and water evaporates. Bill points out that to fill a one pound jar with honey some two million visits to flowerheads have to be made. Such information surprises me and I vow never to look a jar of honey in the eye again without dwelling on this calculation and, indeed, the energy outputs of the little gold-and-black-banded entities involved.

Due to pollen remains found in animal excreta – particularly cave dwellers like hyenas – it is now believed that the relationship between the head of a flower and a worker bee evolved around 100 million years ago.

The bee, bumble or humble, as we know it today pollinates around one fifth of the crops grown in Great Britain. Cauliflowers, broccoli, tomatoes, carrots and apples are all pretty well dependant on bee pollination. Scientists have concluded that bees visually home in on ultraviolet light, thus the smoothness on the inner sides of flower petals direct them instantly to the nectar storage cup. If, for some reason, a flower isn't holding or storing nectar the bee is made aware of this on landing – do they smell it? – and leave without wasting energy.

Population-wise, there are considered to be trillions more honey bees on this planet than there are humans. And two or so thousand flower heads each day are visited by bees from each particular hive grouping.

As I write, and as I speak with Bill, I am in awe of these tiny creatures which we have learned to farm, produce honey crops, much as we have capitalised on most other aspects of farming.

Honey I squirt onto my oats or breakfast cereal every morning but, having first read Edwin Way Teale, have never taken for granted. And along with a honey coating I add grated apple or pear or a few berries. Spraying nectar and pollinating sunshine onto my breakfast is how I look upon it. As for nectar, we often speak of it in the casual way that we do sunshine or rain, but it is definable to my way of thinking in the sense that it is a honey fluid created by flowers. This fluid is indeed yellow.

As for nature's by-product, honeycomb, Bill describes it as 'a waxen structure holding hexagonal cells in which honey and eggs are stored'. And the making of a single honeycomb is surely a wonder within itself?

# JULY

## Wollaton, Nottingham

Withdrawing the curtains, quite often well before 6am, I look out directly onto the branches of my window-side tree and the inhabitants of the avian world are already out there breakfasting. Woodpigeons namely and pausing as if feeling guilty of being caught up here in the branches which is where they belong. Those close to the window pause and study me. Their eyes, bright as gold buttons in the sunlight, their white collars and pink breasts bringing a touch of soft feathered down and beauty to the seasonal eye. Their pale slate grey-blue upper wings devoid of all ruffles suggests immaculate grooming. And so conspicuous and heavy-looking up here amongst the masses of greenery and the small red berry bunches on which they are feeding.

If I remained at the window they would fly heavily and loudly, flapping down to the haw thickets and beyond. There are those amongst them who, having seen me, are turning their heads, seeking escape routes. Because I wish them to remain I withdraw, head into the rooms to prepare my own breakfast.

For the past three weeks – and possibly throughout August – the blackbirds and their broods of the year arrow directly to the cherries, break one off and depart to swallow it in a sanctuary of branches elsewhere. And those 'blackbird arrows' shoot by my window, back and forth, 60 to 80 times a day from the 4.30 daybreak until the 10.15 dusk. Nor are they feeding on these cherries exclusively. They know the whereabouts of fruiting elders, Rowans and blackberries. Consequently, the morning meadow grass earthworms aside, the blackbirds have now each varied diets, berry salads with garden-pillaged gooseberries and raspberries fitting the fill as 'side orders'.

The more ponderous wood pigeons probably eat less in proportion to their size but those maintaining loose territories in the woods just up the road from here will be adding grain, *much grain*, to their field's edge diets.

Last evening a pair had to wait in the upper storey hawthorn thickets until those already ahead of them had fed and vacated their leafy restaurant.

Wood pigeons, however, one doesn't catch sleeping. There is always something for them to do, or be doing, even if that something is only testing the weights of the tree and thicket branches. The pair which were the focal point from the eyrie of my settee were honeymooners, to say the least. The male found a position in the branches a little higher than the female and ensured that his tail was there for the admiring of. Time, time and time again he outfanned that tail. Not a particularly outstanding gesture to my eyes but to those of his mate, or intended mate, the display may have borne the magnificence and intricacy of a displaying male peacock.

At intervals throughout the day, male wood pigeons rise into the air on winnowing wings and dive, shallowly but unmistakably, in mid-air above their perched mates in a bid, I believe, to show off the pink colourations swathing their crops. They make use of the space and the air around them. It is their form of display which, I admit, is limited with the wood pigeon. But it is intriguing nevertheless.

## Runnymede, Surrey (but a month later than I intended)

Around, if not on, 15 June 1215, King John met with his barons in the barons' successful bid to lay down the foundations of the Magna Carta, allegedly here on Runnymede Green.

That sense of bygone pageantry stoking prongs at my imagination again, and last month's television programme – presented and researched by David Starkey – on the subject sharpens my awareness. As a communicator I admire Starkey's direct approach, his aura of assertion, to the extent of me buying his book. Like most interested parties I had the Magna Carta field set out in my imagination. In this Sir Walter Scott-type scenario that lodged so neatly in the cloisters of my mind, the main picture was that of cloaked and bearded men signing documents, perhaps having paragraphs read out to them.

That is until Sir David Starkey pointed out that there is still no evidence to indicate that King John could write. Instead he may have used the Royal Seal with finality. I was thinking along these lines as, having crossed the lovely meadow here, I arrived at the Thames, alongside which in recent years I have strolled the path between Windsor and Staines. The notebook writer re-enters my head. Five unfamiliar shapes – wood duck in eclipse – preen and oil on the grass at the water's edge. To my eyes they are unfamiliar because we do not get them to any noticeable degree up in the Midlands. This group consists of a duck and her four surviving 'flappers' which, in six weeks when the eclipse or moult period is complete, will resemble their parents in appearance.

Here in Surrey the species is at home among riverine backwaters, ponds and wooded ridges. Usually the mated pairs nest in tree holes, perhaps at Runnymede in the ruinous bough hole of a Cooper's Hill Wood oak.

A clutch of 15 or 16 eggs results in about a dozen ducklings after an incubation period of between 28 to 31 days; and, in the way of the city block nesting mallard, the duck calls them down to the ground when she is ready to take them to the water.

At Runnymede the brood cross, I would think, the meadow before the grass and buttercup stems are high. But over the next weeks spent exploring the bays and reed beds of the Thames's edge, the ducklings will have fallen foul of gulls, crows, pike and mink. Consequently, the little family preening a few feet from me are typical in that – the mink aside – such a small proportion of this average brood may now well reach adulthood. A breeder of ornamental ducks incidentally assures me that by the time she is one year old a duck of the species can lay a clutch of fertile eggs.

Upslope in Cooper's Hill Wood daylight flying moths pebbledash the oak glades, but, again largely due to the moult and change of the year, the songbirds have fallen silent. Both species of pied woodpecker use the wood on their 'flight line' journeys across country, and the more residential nuthatches would have been singing at their lustiest back in May.

It is linnet, lark and bunting country this noticeably sloped tract of historic England, where the Air Force memorial commemorating the lives of 20,000 men and women who – British or not – faced the German Advance Lines and lost their lives far from the graveyards of their natal parishes.

Below Cooper's Hill Wood also stands a colonnade, domed and called the Magna Carta Memorial. I first viewed this shortly after it was erected in 1957. I was an RAF conscript based at Abingdon in Berkshire and the RAF laid on an occasional weekend bus for us conscripts who were otherwise 'weekending' at our base.

Standing beside this memorial almost sixty years later I recalled my unit having to move to a set of billets at nearby Culham shortly after our visit. Here in the autumn I used to shave in the cabin-style toilets and washrooms block while listening to acorns raining down from the surrounding oaks and thudding onto the tarpaulined roof above my head.

Living in these billets was my closest experience to 'cabin fever', about which I have since read, and – harsh winters to come or no harsh winters to come – I could quite take to living that way full time, even though old age is appearing on my lifeline horizon.

The RAF memorial was presented and erected by the American Bar Association, and nearby stands a great pale block that is, in fact, a monolith to J F Kennedy. For minutes I was thrown and asking myself whether or not this was the place for such monuments to be erected. But later, after a further meadow stroll to the Magna Carta tea room, I had pointed out to me the fact that the American Constitution was founded on the exact principles of the Magna Carta. And so there, at a little coffee table, I *learnt something* that day that I hadn't even considered in my foolish, but free-ranging, days as an RAF conscript.

In and around the Magna Carta villages of Egham and Englefield, I expect there are folk who could name all the wildflowers that swathe the meadow in May, along with the different types of grasses, insects, hoverflies and bees and, with that point in mind, I resolve to return next May perhaps with a notebook, camera and the hand of friendship extended towards anyone who would care to accommodate me for a few days.

## Wollaton, Nottinghamshire

The months of summer host uncomfortable conditions which bring on hay fever and asthma to unfortunate sufferers. I detest humid evenings when the whitish grey sky gives nothing away but remains resolute, brooding. Yet when, often close to midnight, thunder weather rolls its cannons out onto the battlefields of the sky, I am tempted to become a room-ensconced spectator.

The most recent midnight storm I couldn't have slept through anyway. Moreover the creative within me refused to sleep and insisted that I take a pad and pen out to the two-storeyed living room and kitchen to record something of what was taking place. As the heated flares of lightnings zigzagged, with thunderclaps soon following, so descended the rain. Drenching and cool.

Moths and bats had surely sought shelter? Young birds, that were mere entities forming in eggshells three or four months back, would be cowered, perched low in the underbush, frightened, wide-eyed and attempting perhaps to seek others of their own species.

Wood pigeons, magpies, jackdaws had probably already set roosting positions in the evergreen pines and garden cypresses. The tawny, little and barn owls would have returned to their nesting holes and niches. But there would be feathered casualties amongst the young and inexperienced nevertheless.

As the storm swept in with its rain curtains so too did words attempting to describe aspects of it emerge from the nib of my Biro as I alternately sipped water from a mug on the kitchen worktop.

*... Catatone Hill on the horizon*
*became swiftly washed by swathings*
*of black and red*
*obliterated in both shape and presence*

*by the brushes and sprays of the*
*storm vandal riding in on that wind...*
*Every charged bayonet of lightning, clap of thunder,*
*varies like the faces of people one passes daily*
*in the street...*

*Curtains of much-needed rain took precedence,*
*the stage of the sky in darkness to the north*
*yielded to increasing light as uncomfortably*
*close blue tongues of lightning, lethal,*
*intent and startling, demanded an audience.*

*To the west the lightning forks flared vivid red,*
*stoked by the reflected embers of the sunset.*
*Red lightning through one window,*
*blue the other windows.*
*Dominating mind, eye and increasing pulse.*

*Blue-banded cars were slowly driven*
*through sheets of blue-banded rain.*
*The pounding of rain on windows,*
*the conquering darkness with its*
*deadly fusings of natural electricity*
*all out there.*

*Thunder cannonaded directly overhead,*
*the lightning scalpels repeatedly sliced the sky,*
*some incisions clearly divided,*
*others zigzagged. Dramatically misshapen.*

'Never seen colours like them' a friend agreed when we met for coffee the next day. I later learned that 14 miles south, at the home of another friend, the lights went out for three minutes.

Throughout the rest of that following day we learned of the carnage and saw television footage of roofless houses. We learned of a boy targeted by a lethal band of lightning as he hurried home across a sports field. Learned also of cows sheltering beneath fieldside trees but within seconds those cows were reduced to huge lumps of cinder flesh.

Locally, then, every living thing was at the mercy of that tri-coloured extravagance. Every living thing or something connected to it. Sullen, brooding, *overheating*, July can suddenly unleash its furies in this way.

And all we humans can do is wait.

Following such storms those harvesting hope that the clouds move on and the land dries out quickly. The crops have been growing since April and throughout May and June.

Too much rain results in collapsing long-stemmed crops – such as oats, wheat and barley – dependant, of course, upon the soils across which they have been sown.

When I was about ten I saw from a coach window field crops that were turned black due to weather devastation, and my mother explained that the reason was largely due to the rainfalls that had been unusually heavy for midsummer. On our calendars and in our diaries St Swithin's Day reminds us that we could have 40 days of rain. Not that I have ever believed it any more than I believed, by the age of nine, the parable about 'The Feeding of the Five Thousand' on five loaves and two little fishes. One *has* to be joking, sir or madam.

However, if it remains dry and humid around – or on – St Swithin's Day then those conditions could still remain for some 40 days. The droughts of the 1970s proved the folklorists right but we were, after all, experiencing the farmer's harvesting calender weeks of midsummer.

The Dog Star, or Sirius, is now above us, although, in truth, I could only pick out The Plough for anyone if I was challenged. But, due to this star, the days co-existing beneath it are often referred to as 'The Dog Days of Summer' hereabout. Muggy weather, when one seems to break into a sweat at every turn of the head, is unpleasant for most of us, but we endure it. Do we have a choice?

Most village cottages and suburban buildings needing weatherproofing or renovation are to be seen at this time of year with scaffolding, workmen, lorries parked and tilers hard at work around them.

Swallows and house martins flick around objects with enviable dexterity and even breach the wind draughts and spin drifts otherwise created by high-sided vehicles and heavy traffic. The swallows are able to turn away from an otherwise lethal collision, as if calculating distance and the force of the prevailing wind or breeze all at the same time, with the ease and precision of an instinct that, to my mind, is the human equivalent of acting upon the requests of roadside traffic signs installed for humans.

They are superb aerialists and use those instinctive twists and turns to secure the flying insects upon which they feed. Do they ever *miss* an insect on the wing? We will never know. But I doubt it. Which is probably why evolution has designed them that way. Streamlined lightweights that speed through life with an instinctive zest that, in the cooler months ahead, will see them crossing to the Mediterranean countries. Here in Britain many swallows and house martins roost in reed beds prior to their departure. But there are few among we enthusiasts who see them finally depart.

Already the ploughs are out across the fields as – with the oilseed rape harvest safely in storage – the furrows for next year's crop are already patterning the landscapes. However, there is still much stubble to be ploughed over and the rooks – with their local populations swollen by the young of the year – seek insects on both ploughland and stubble from daybreak to dusk.

On a village grass verge one hot morning I disturbed a family of jackdaws sunbathing – passing traffic regardless – and the young I could barely tell apart from the breeding pair.

The grassy ridges and sheep pastures now host the pale forms of shorn sheep that may later be turned out to feed on the fields which have nurtured root crops.

In the winter those fields currently holding sheep will be grazed by wigeon duck and mute swans, often in good number because those birds are attracted to the oil substance which emanates from the bodies of sheep and coats the ground with what I think of as being 'greasy grass'. And in thinking thus, I'm reminded that the Native Americans would also have referred to vacated sheep pasture by the same name, or a name close to it.

But do the swans and the wigeon actually smell the 'greasy grass' when they are in the vicinity? Or do the local swan pairs earmark those tracts of pasture, close to rivers and waterways, as places which may sustain them calcium-wise throughout the winter months? We don't know, can only surmise. But what I *do* know is that riverside sheep pasture is never left untouched. Mute swans, and perhaps wintering families of whooper and Bewick, always flock in to graze it. They are undergoing their winter 'greasy grass' *fixes.*

One of the first trees to remind us that the year is maintaining its cycle is the Rowan or mountain ash. The name Rowan derives from a Norse word meaning red, or in Gaelic 'Ruadhan' the red ore.

The berries in midsummer show a ripening skin texture of orange which will deepen to red. Two months before the berries are properly ripe the blackbirds and wood pigeons, not to mention a magpie or two, are visiting and have given my window-side cherry tree a respite.

The stands of flowering and ripening blackberries and raspberries will be sampled next by these birds.

# AUGUST

## West Midlands Lay-By

Journeying to the West Midlands following a brief trek around a foothill escarpment in the Shropshire hill country, a friend and I pulled into a side lane and with time to spare we strolled a bracken-edged track to a tract of walled woodland overlooking a shallow, disused quarry.

There were a cluster of living vans in the quarry base and a broad-shouldered man, who could be taken for an experienced mountaineer, waving and calling out 'good morning'.

Turning with the wall path we had soon the bracken and quarry tilting west on our right. Ahead a farm gate, loop chained and exclaiming 'No Further Please', ended our stroll but so splendid were the stands of foxgloves that I decided to take a couple of photographs, especially as their bell-shaped petals were luring in bees, each for a nectar-lifting investigation.

A past colleague, Tony Perkins – and past in the sense that we haven't met for some twenty years – always rolled out its Latin name *Digitalis purpurea*, which I found as fascinating a name as he.

The stalks or stems resemble spikes, and what appear to be the inner 'tongues' are whitish pink speckled with black. Does this arrangement draw in bees and flying insects and, if so, for what purposes other than to collect nectar-like substances? Come to think of it can bees, wasps, hoverflies and such see colours in the same ways as ourselves?

Having taken a couple of camera studies, I paused to take in all that we had around: a track made by humans and, perhaps long ago, bridle-led ponies; bracken fronds by the thousand, almost the height of our elbows; foxgloves; bees; and, on our left, a low but definitive stone wall laid by, *built by*, humans; while before us the five-barred gate had been assembled, again by humans – possibly one human – a craftsman, carpenter, builder in every sense of the term. The wall carried on sloping down, but without a stone or boulder missing, to the highest ledge of the old quarry.

So much to see. And, glory be! Not a crisp packet or discarded carrier bag in sight.

Determined not to be left out of our scrutiny, a male wren sprang onto an upright of the farm gate and burst into song. How far away? Ten feet. In his bouts of song the wren may have been warning his mate and scattered family that a potential intruder was prowling in their little corner of Great Britain.

The bill agape, red inner throat showing and tiny tongue throbbing as it conducted the entire orchestration from within the rostrum of that throat, the wren tuned to the extent of us seeing its entire rotund body quivering. The deep chestnut feathers, *russet*, edged with black, were sheened due to the little bird's long bouts of sprucing and preening. The pert tail, suggestive of stiff feathers but with short tail held upright, as I'm sure everyone in the world must know, was equally groomed.

The tiny pink-toed feet were outspread on the gate support, fragile-looking but used as climbing irons or crampons when the wren ascends the stone walls and tree trunks in its bid to fashion and furnish several domed-shaped nests, which, by now, would be vacated by his one or two broods but perhaps used as roosts when the hard weather sets in.

A flip and flash of russet grey wings and the wren was gone, but with its song stored in the archives of our minds.

So much to see on one short walk and every short walk if one uses his or her eyes. And *heard* if the hearing is not impaired. In every unknown 'somewhere' there is to be found something of natural interest. And in our case that day all for the pulling in at an out-of-the-way layby.

## Dorset

Dorset enthusiast and photographer, Peter, has investigated further into the growing and harvesting of opium poppies, I learn over our evening pints of bitter.

To grow these poppies in Great Britain the agriculturist needs a Home Office Licence but the variety sown is used, *and indeed useful*, as part of a pharmaceutical morphine which needs an articulate refining process – *a good deal of refining* – to extract the ingredients that will result in morphine.

In 2014 the record harvest for opium poppies was achieved, and eastern and southern England have the best soil and climate conditions to get such harvests under way. However, we are not talking about illicit drug use here apparently because the type of seed sown on these soils doesn't allow for that. Opium is not an *immediate* process but, on a final note, I was further surprised to learn that 50 per cent of the morphine now used by the medical and pharmaceutical professions is grown here in England.

## Wollaton, Nottinghamshire

Here in a month which we think of as being the peak of summer with its sense of steadiness, deep foliage and fruiting berries, the pulse of migration is seething within the instinctive guidance modes of the swift and cuckoo. To these birds the warmer climes are calling; the need to use their wings to their fullest advantage pleading to be exorcised. And the remarkable thing is that the swifts, of the year's egg-pierced intake, and the more solitary inclined cuckoos, each answer to a given instinctive direction that connects them to where they should be but where, *as yet*, many of their numbers have not yet been. Incredible, yet seeming as natural to the birds involved as the movements needed to enable them to flit from one tree branch to another. Nor do we see them go.

On the land the agriculturists are harvesting and ploughing, taking every advantage of the dry long spells and using the hours accordingly. There is no 9.30 start for these people. They work flexi-time, yes, but the work clock begins at first light, still soon after 5.30am.

Hereabout there is some considerable cross shuttling of harvested crops. Perhaps related farmers buying or striking up business arrangements with each other, and it is usually in the relative quiet of the sunlit evenings that huge, elongated lorries travel the main roads out this way, journeying from the rich meadowlands in the south to the Derbyshire foothills country in the north and west. When I see these transporters at sunset I think back to those seventy or eighty years ago when – according to books and monochrome film reels – the harvesters journeyed home in carts pulled by Shire or Suffolk Punch horses, the grown-ups walking beside the carts and the children often riding on the peaks of the great sunset-enhanced harvest of gold.

I can't remember when I last cried openly. Fifty years ago probably. But late one recent afternoon I was suddenly reduced to tears as my ears transferred me to the infant school classroom. This state of affairs came about when two schoolgirls passing along the lane below my windows burst into their own lovely duetted rendition of 'The Song of Harvest Home'. This hymn, or whatever we may care to call it, stirs this old atheist as no other and has always remained my favourite. As they sang – and as *we* sang in the school assembly halls – I thought of the people from the past whose lives had revolved around the fields and the seasons of the year.

The so-called land-working families, or *serfs,* who knew no life other than the workhouse, if hard times fell upon them. They knew toil, hard work, severe weather conditions and abject poverty. And each were offered a lifespan of forty or fifty years. Many of them never saw or went to towns and cities, even less read the morning newspaper with a cappuccino smiling on the table in front of them. And their 'special day of the week' was Sunday when they were expected, by the Squire, to attend at least one church service.

They are there in the very first sentence of 'The Song of Harvest Home'.

'Sing, ye grateful people, sing…'

And if the season had been good they were *grateful.* To the weather and the conditions of the land. A very different people from those that we know in Great Britain today. *A very different people.*

They lived *with* and *for* the land. And knew little or nothing beyond that way of life. At the village schools they had learned reading, writing and arithmetic with perhaps an occasional history lesson or physical training session thrown in for good measure. When time allowed they played in the village streets and at dusk followed the old village lamplighter on his rounds.

The church, with its pews, altar and hymn books, they knew like the backs of their hands. And, sadly, they were not expected to know much more except perhaps how to back a horse into the shafts of a cart or milk the Squire's cows.

We pass their earth-ensconced remains when we drive by a village church, in these times usually graced by mature yew or sweet and horse-chestnut trees which, in summer, often hide the solidarity of the bell-tower.

They are each beneath a stone – often sunken deep into the earth – forgotten and, in many cases, unrecorded. But these generations were those who, with a parochial sincerity, sang 'The Song of Harvest Home', their anthem. One old lady who saw the end of those times lived in a toll road cottage at the crossroads situated barely a quarter of a mile from here.

There is a small covert-type wood planted on each corner of these roads but, explore though I have, I cannot find the remains of a bygone dwelling. Not even a layer of house bricks to suggest a pig-sty. But there is in existence a photograph of this lady in what could only be her 'Sunday best'. And I have a copy.

To those who were nearing their dotage around the time that I was born, she was known as 'Grannie Simmonds'. Looking at the photograph it is difficult to think of her as a young girl. Her background and her husband's employment are not on record. But she was born to a family whose job it was – the wife usually – to charge tolls to vehicles such as carts, gigs and carriers' carts passing along that way from one town or city to another.

The photograph depicts Grannie Simmonds wearing a dark blouse and long skirt to a small jacket, and the type of flat hat that can only be described as a skullcap.

Although she would have been paid by whoever owned the road or nearest land boundary at that time, she lived off the land as best she could.

Gamekeeper and poacher would call on her carrying a brace of pheasants, rabbits or wood pigeon. She would never divulge the whereabouts of the biggest sweet chestnuts that she used to roast in her hearth, and the recipe for her locally famed pickled walnuts she gave to no one either.

She also carried a recipe for curing corns, using ivy leaves, and also warts.

Attached to the cottage was a small orchard and from the apple, pear and plum trees she collected these fruits on the warm evenings at summer's end, placed them in buckets and the next day carried the buckets down to the canal bridge. Here she placed the laden buckets in the undergrowth close to the bridge and returned later to find that the long and narrowboat people – carrying their consignments of coal – had taken the fruits as expected and filled the lined buckets with lumps of coal in exchange.

On other occasions, Grannie Simmonds left garden vegetables, eggs and an occasional table-ready plucked chicken for the boat people.

She was apparently to be seen in the woods collecting kindling every day, and, in the summer, if she saw or was told about a group of children picking wildflowers Grannie Simmonds appeared before them wearing a conical hat, shrieking and waving her stick. And not surprisingly the children thought they were being accosted by a witch! They ran!

Grannie Simmonds' attire then tells us from the photograph that she had *some* form of income, slightly above the ordinary for those times. But my guess is that she was younger than her facial features suggest. But at least I would imagine her skin to have been weathered. However, the photograph of another lady suggests, in her particular case, anything but this. The photograph I am referring to is that of the mother of D H Lawrence, which is currently on display in the novelist's birthplace at Eastwood in Nottinghamshire. Life-wearied and work worn, Lawrence's mother on the photograph looks almost twice her age.

People may argue that genetics have a lot to do with it. Well, quite so. But a rigorous daily routine – such as many women experienced during those times – would also take its toll on their health, surely?

In truth I was shocked when I viewed the photograph. Shocked and saddened. Nor did D H Lawrence himself live to what might today be called a grand old age.

The majority, wherever they were situated, turned to the church. Moreover they were *expected* to be seen amongst the assembly. And at this time of the year, as in the spring – the season of seed sowing – they sang for *and to* the yields of the land around which their lifestyles were interwoven.

The first lines of that lovely hymn say it all.

In this, the last full month of summer, a sense of full foliaged peace is conveyed to the eye, especially when we see the herds of red deer stags or fallow bucks couched in silhouette beneath such widespreading trees as the horse- and sweet-chestnut.

In the forested areas they use the pines to seek the shade and also the stands of oak, or black poplar.

Whether wild or emparked, the antlers of these magnificent beasts appear twice as majestic now due to their thickness because from April until August the antlers have been protected by a layer of growth skin that is known as 'velvet'. But now, with the year moving on, the velvet needs to be shed for the antlers of each stag are fully developed and will be used as combative aids in the oncoming 'rut' or mating season. Like the harvests of our fruit and tree nurseries, our crops and wildflower meadows, the growth of a pair of antlers culminates in the genetic pattern, size and width and ceases when each stag tentatively rubs the antler tines, main beams and tops against fence posts, heather tufts or overhangs of tree foliage and in the space of two or three days sheds the entire 'velvet' covering.

The stags are then said to be 'clean of velvet' or 'in hard antler' and the entire process – since the previous pair of antlers was shed the previous March or April – takes 16 weeks, if the stag is a matured beast.

All through the summer the antlers, and any bloodied wounds made on them, have fallen prey to hordes of gnats, midges and flies that swarm in to feed on the blood. These pests have laid eggs in the nostrils and ear cavities of the stags and capitalised on any form of liquidation or similar moist substances. Seed heads have also played their parts in irritating the stags when they have been feeding in deep, long-stemmed grasses or passing through bracken, which is why, as the summer months move on, stags usually seek out flat grassed and even roadside pasture if it is within their respective orbits.

The dominant or 'master' stags can weigh 230 to 250lbs at the time of the velvet stripping. In our deer-parks a stag with strips of velvet temporarily hampering its full field of vision may be fractious to the point of aggression if humans stray close, which is understandable. In the wild a stag similarly handicapped will seek deep cover until it is completely clear of the velvet.

As the weeks of the rut nudge towards the onset of autumn, many park-bred stags display little or no fear of humans. The fact that their antlers have reached full culmination is also an indication that the stags are loaded with testosterone and its associated aggression. Having known park-bred stags for some seventy years, I seldom stray to within 20 or 30 feet of them. There have been occasions when I have foolishly strayed within a stag's orbit, or have needed to to carry out my duties.

Not infrequently a stag has taken a few trotting steps in my direction but halted when I moved aside. One individual lows cow-like through its nostrils in the present herd and I heed the sign accordingly. And twice – quite some years ago – I unwittingly withdrew from two separate stags a vocal warning that was not only new to me but other enthusiasts. I needed to work at a hand-gate, alongside which an eight-year-old stag was grazing. Assuming that a direct approach would move the stag aside I strode to the gate, at which move the stag ceased its grazing, lifted its head so that the antlers were laid tines upward along its dorsal ridge and, with its eyes rolling and mouth agape, gave vent to a series of singular clicking sounds that emanated from the back of its throat. The stag was making its point and its stand.

On the second occasion one of a stag trio walking in file, but which were closely approached by sightseers, adopted a similar defensive routine and the visitors took heed of my warning.

In the shade, then, stags can be seen couched and chewing the cud. Stags, whose respective ages are recognisable due to their body sizes and antler widths and varied developments, still remain together. Make no mistake, each young three- or four-year-old stag knows its own position within that cervine hierarchy. If a master stag approaches the shade of the tree it will make for the shadiest spot. If this is occupied by a younger stag the dominant stag will stride directly towards that spot, at which move the younger stag will usually rise and give way to its superior. The superior exercises that riveting gait while swaying almost imperceptibly from side to side, thus using his shadow, if he is still in sunlight, to emphasise his bulk.

The dominant stag will also use the shadow effect when, out on the grazing land, he approaches a less dominant stag feeding heartily on a grass tuft. The subordinate stag must smell the dominant beast approaching – his urine, secretion scent and semen – and also, due to the sideways placed eyes of a deer, see the shadow closing in. Thus, before he is badly gored about the flanks, the subordinate stag will step away and not return.

I never cease to be intrigued by the fact that stags, at a nettle bed, will stand in a row facing inwards and bite off the many nettle heads which the chewing motions of their jaws suggest are quite succulent to these magnificent animals with their extensive palates.

Red deer will also swim and wade regularly in water, feeding on reed stems, floating carpets of duckweed and water lilies, particularly during the moisture-declining weeks at summer's end.

## Leicestershire Wolds

There are still fields of barley to be brought in. Golden stalked, resolute and upright in some areas; bleached, as if exhausted by the heat, in others. Around the crop field peripheries flowers, such as the camomile and wild poppies, provide frames of colour for the seasonal eye.

On the thistle heads soldier beetles – bright red like splashes of blood – live out their life cycles, and the brown and orange gatekeeper butterflies tenant the umbellifers and sunbathe on the rungs of farm gates.

Combine harvesters are steadily driven – rotation fashion – across the productive contours of land, forcing hares, foxes and roe deer to break from cover.

Cylindrical hay bales, wrapped and early weatherproofed, await departure to the storage sheds.

Two kestrels hover above the harvest fields, they are scanning for disturbed rodents or small birds. A gauze of grey momentarily screens the skyscape, swifts perhaps on their migrational journeys south. But the redstarts, whinchats, reed and sedge warblers will also soon be crossing country and channel, but under the stars perhaps. Who amongst us can say?

Under normal circumstances the stubble fields frequented by rooks, lapwing, wood pigeons and gulls do not remain as stubble fields for long. The agriculturists are soon there sowing them early with grass, which, if drilled early into the ground, can take a good hold before the months of cold, wet weather merge in.

A quick growing crop are stubble turnips, which are often sown directly into the stubble before it is ploughed over. Stubble turnips also get a quick hold and in the height of winter provide a green calcium source for our sheep flocks.

Winter wheat follows and the oily textured oilseed rape. In a relatively dry season, beans and winter wheat settle into the nurseries of the soil.

By the middle of May, at the end of each sowing year, the last of the crops will be in the earth and now, in August, the lorries and trailers – loaded with varied crops, hay and straw – are on the roads, some consignments heading for relatively long-distant destinations, but the majority more localised and short – probably land share arrangements exchanged between farming families and relatives.

As for the land yield itself, wheat is considered to be the most nutritious of our cereal crops. There are several varieties but basically wheat is the golden grain culmination that gathers beneath the sky on an upright stalk. The best quality varieties are used for milling from which processed flour results for the bread and confectionery industries. Breakfast cereals derive, of course, from these good-quality varieties. Wheat which is considered to be of less quality goes to feed livestock and is therefore, not surprisingly, called 'feed wheat'. Besides animal livestock it is also fed to game birds, such as pheasants and partridges, in their rearing pens.

Wheat, then, is high protein and surpasses all other cereal crops. The stalks from it, however, are less durable and are collectively used as bedding straw for quartering stables, cow feeding sheds and lambing pens. That lovely warm smell emanating from the stockyard or stable block is straw interlaced with animal dung which will eventually be put back onto the land.

A by-product of wheat is bran, which feeds both animals and humans. And, although we think so little about it and take our bread loaves on the supermarket shelves for granted, our lives, and indeed the health of each average person amongst us, would be so much the poorer without it.

# SEPTEMBER

## Wollaton Nr Nottingham

Imperceptibly the autumn eases into the scene like a character that has been waiting in the soap opera wings for a script writer team to develop it. Except that this month needs no developing in the sense of a becalmed transition bridging the gap between the summer and the more colourful but colder months ahead.

Suburban roads are again crammed with early morning traffic as the colleges and schools return to teaching centre, classroom and laboratory, and the first sprays of golden leaf become backlit by the morning light.

It was with a sense of trepidation gnawing at my mind that, in the 1940s, I walked to the infant school wondering whose and what number class I would be required to attend on that first school morning in September.

I walked to school beside regiments of lime trees. Consequently, the leaves and the strengthening wind were my companions as the earth tilted slightly away from the sun.

I would always hope that the teacher whose class I would be drafted into would maintain the all-important nature table. And usually she did. Especially Miss Gibson.

In September the heads of oats, wheat and barley would be arranged and labelled so that each child knew which crop type they were looking at. I always added a used blackbird's nest, alongside the nest of a song thrust, pointing out that the latter lined its nest solely with mud whereas the more industrious blackbirds added a good layer of dried grass over the mud lining.

I also took frogspawn and, as children, we watched the tadpoles develop.

Miss Gibson lined a pound jam-jar with pink blotting paper and between that and the glass eased the seed of a runner bean in to face the light. And, sure enough, within weeks the runner bean responded by sprouting green shoots.

Having a nature table in the classroom served as a reminder to us all that life was throbbing at full pitch beyond the classroom and always had been and always would be. Entities died but others were born, hatched or germinated to replace them. And consistently.

A further successful attempt by my school to bridge the gap between people and nature occurred each Monday afternoon when we trooped into a classroom as potential listeners to a BBC radio broadcast for children. The scripts were enhanced, in many cases by wildlife recordings made by the BBC's first sound recordist Dr Ludwig Koch. His fascinating autobiography *Memoirs of a Birdman*, published in 1955, is still to be located today within an arm's length of my writing desk.

Each broadcast was scheduled in a school's wildlife and environment magazine. That way we youngsters studied the grey seals on Skomer Island; the mobbing skuas; portly resolute puffins; and a variety of gulls while we were listening to them calling with slight, but never extensive, interventions administered by a narrator who was not always Dr Ludwig Koch.

There was always a coloured photograph on the cover of the magazines which accompanied the programme, and in my mind I can see the photograph on the first edition still some seventy years after I first rested it on my lap.

The photograph was that of one of the black-backed gulls, probably a lesser, standing over its roughly made nest and clutch of four blotched eggs. I recall the 'cold' expressionless orb of the gull's eye, the pinkish legs and webbed feet and noting that the eggs were placed narrow end inwards to the centre of the nest.

The schools of Britain then seemed to be in close touch, *liaison*, with the BBC, but being a youngster I had no idea then how the involvement came about any more than I have today.

Our particular school, if not others, was also – magazine-wise – involved with the RSPCA and for a small sum of money we could purchase that society's monthly or quarterly publication *Animal Ways*.

There was little to do with wildlife in those early editions except swans; a photograph depicting two small cygnets riding in the safety cradle of a pen's wings an advisory piece on what to do if we lads saw a swan sitting on the surface of a frozen waterway. The swan may not have been frozen in. That being the case it was best, safety-wise, if its rescuers laid a ladder on the frozen surface of the water and used the rungs as they would were they ascending to a part of a building.

The foregoing, then, is an attempt to interpret the fact that the schools in Britain were close to nature – as indeed were the Girl Guides and Boy Scouts – during and just after the years of the Second World War.

Today we have clued-up youngsters with technological equipment working for nature and wildlife habitats throughout our County Trusts, the Wetlands and Wildfowl Trust, Royal Society for the Protection of Birds, the Canal and River Trust, and various other organisations. The countryside although continually threatened is in more young and expert hands than most of us imagine.

Finally, I should mention a young woman conservationist whose name I have never known and with whom I have seldom spoken. A digger of trenches, layer of hedgerows, pollarder of trees, clearer of ditches and maintainer of wildflower meadows.

She has a son. When he was about seven I noticed, as she walked him in my direction, that the young mother had him feel sprigs of grass, overhangs of leaves and the circumference and texture of a tree bole which they came alongside. I said nothing, it was not my place to be interfering. But their respective contacts with the natural world was spirit-lifting to say the least.

## Woodlinkin, Derbyshire

Gossamer, as I understand it, is created by the webs of small spiders, either floating or encasing. And I have always – like dew – associated gossamer with the early mornings, which is why I was so surprised to see the hedgerow of a Derbyshire lane connecting the small roadside community of Woodlinkin with the valley bottom lake known as Loscoe Dam and Furnace Lane. At 3.00-ish on that particularly cool but sunlit afternoon both hedgerows plunging down from the Serpentine ridge road were embalmed with a filmy, breeze-light substance of silver, the likes of which, for all my countryside wanderings, I had not seen to such a pleasantly startling capacity.

The word 'ethereal' sprang to mind, followed by the realisation that, because I was accompanying a friend to a car maintenance unit, I had left the camera back home.

Gossamer is floated, silvered by cool air conditions, flimsy and when seen en masse resembles a natural tapestry created by gauze. A child, out walking with his or her parents that afternoon, could be forgiven for thinking they were on a route heading down into Fairyland. There was, however, a girl coming up the lane in our direction. Florid-cheeked and with hair auburn to the point of reminding me of the outer shell of a sweet-chestnut, she walked waving her hands around in attempts to dissuade tiny parachutes of gossamer from settling their spidery chills onto her cheeks and into her hair.

So how many spiders were involved in this almost dreamworld-type transition? I would think millions if not billions. And how do they survive? Many must feed our hedgerow birds and probably other spiders, flies and larger insects. They are there and, species-wise, must always have been there. There? Well, along almost every tract of hedgeline in Great Britain. Yet, until such conditions as we were experiencing that afternoon occurred, we, or anyone, never thought of them being in existence, let alone spinning tiny yet eye-catching webs throughout our hedgerows.

"What is it? What's causing all this?" asked the laughing blue-eyed girl. Her hair, eyelids and cheeks were wet due to her trek through the gossamer forest. Yes, she walked the lane regularly but had never seen it so bejewelled, so out of the ordinary.

"A unique experience," I assured her.

Yet a change in temperature, as the dusk came in, could alter matters completely. And, who knows, we agreed tomorrow it could be raining.

## Calke Abbey, South Derbyshire

Oak rides and the avenues of our manorial parklands I never miss visiting in the autumn. The more sequestered the better.

I stroll and if a fallen tree is available I sit and wait; and watch. Red and fallow deer feed on the calcium-enriched acorns and continually descending drifts of beech mast. Pheasants likewise. Jays, so colourful even against the first layers of copper leaves enshrouding the grass and tree roots, feed singularly. Or, if paired, slightly apart seeking acorns and – like the grey or red squirrels – burying those that they regard as surplus, yet will not dispense with entirely.

In such rides or avenues – especially on a frost-smarting daybreak or dusk – the tangible scents of leaf decay pleasantly infiltrate the nostrils. The musk is there on the threads of a breeze. Woody, like old worn teak, or alternating with the suggestion of damp, *wet* sawdust. No human being has a recipe for this concoction. Were it a dish on a menu it might well be called 'Autumn Trifle'. But it is there to tantalise not the taste buds but the nostrils.

The gamekeepers of times gone by must have worked with these drifting delights enhancing the backgrounds of their woodland glade workshops every year of their occupational lives. Moreover these scents of September and October would have crept imperceptibly into the rooms of their cottages, their woodsheds and across garden vegetable plots.

Their domestic hens, like the pheasants, would scratch harder and longer with their feet into the layers of leaf mould to pick up insects or torpid insect forms and overlooked seeds.

Life; it is throbbing and thriving everywhere, even on the sea bed.

But, fortunately for me, not many folk appreciate the September delights of an oak ride. Which is why, when I seek them out, I prefer to be alone.

## Church Wilne, South Derbyshire
## 'the church amongst the willows'

Walking the margins of the gravel-extraction lakes my son alerts me to the spectacle of a swallow group, probably at the beginnings of their migrational journey, being shadowed by a hobby falcon – a winged cloud playing the dicing-with-death game against the splendour of the sunset.

All movement, all flickering wings, swerving, changing formation, repositions and, from the swallows, excitable twitterings. But the hobby falcon is undeterred and will probably roost in the reed beds with this swallow group and the hundreds of other Hirundinidae – swallows, house and sand martins – which will join them for an overnight stay.

As the concourse swells across country, ocean and continent so more hobby falcons will join, parasite and prey on the swallows and martins. Like migrating animal herds, the hobbies move with their main source species for survival and return to Britain with them.

The hobbies will feed on other small birds, insects, worms and may attempt to tackle small rodents. But while there are flocks of swallows and martins there will be hobby falcons flying in close predatory attendance.

Furrows created by the blades of a plough. Dark soil *earth* being brought to the ground surface to face the sky. Black-headed gulls, jackdaws and, infrequently, a heron follow the paths made by the plough blades to feed upon the insect life disorientated by the earth movements; the gulls – bickering, lifting and lowering – squabbling as they capitalise on all that was safe and below ground the previous day.

I visit ploughing matches, the top prizes being awarded to those who can plough the straightest furrow. Social occasions, a chance for true countrymen to get together. A reminder – as we look at the teams of horses – of the ploughmen of the past, many suffering from curvature of the spine as they reached their prime, having to walk 11 to 15 miles a day behind the horses, the sudden downpours of rain regardless.

If the site allows there may be a show ring. A small gymkhana for the young, local pony club equestrians, perhaps followed by the parade of a county's foxhound pack.

There are mushrooms on the fields and wide varieties of fungi flourishing on the tree trunks. And the seasonal eye becomes accustomed to seeing leaves... drifting... drifting... imperceptibly from the deciduous tree branches. By day and by night. Drifting, drifting.

Pause now and inhale. Take in the aromas of the land, the scents of the woodland tracts. Get some aspect of the autumn inside of you.

## Savernake Forest, Wiltshire

The russets of the leaf sprays are enhanced by raindrops bejewelled by sunlight; the paths slotted by the cloven hoofprints of fallow deer that used them in their nocturnal quests for acorns and beech mast.

The air quality on such mornings as this, and in the glades of our ancient forests, comes over almost as if it has been kept in a cooler overnight.

And the sense of civilisation is gone. The motorways, even the B roads, non-existent, still to emerge in the centuries of the future. We have stepped back in time.

I would think the forest here regenerated from heathland. But, in the sense of human ownership, the trees had matured sufficiently by the twelfth and thirteenth centuries for the extensive acreage to be regarded as Crown Land.

A forest was the hunting ground of a king. A 'chase' the hunting ground of an earl. A king could hunt over the chase without the earl's permission. But the earl had to seek the king's permission before he could hunt in the forest. We are talking 1086 and beyond here.

Deer were retained and encouraged to thrive in the forest, whereas other animals were, where possible, fenced out. Thus the term 'park' or 'parke' came into existence. Park – 'the place where the deer are kept'.

Lawns for the deer to graze across were also founded and pollarded thickets – like the haw and blackthorn – were well managed with regard to providing the deer species with calcium.

Rides – grassy, wide strips of land – were cut through most forests in order for the mounted 'verderers' or forest keepers to regularly patrol and, of course, to further provide hunting access for the king and his entourage.

A villager whom we met just before we entered the forest today told us that many of the oaks dated from the seventeenth century in Savernake. A second or third generation of oaks, then, I would imagine. Whether these many oaks were *planted by* the seventeenth century or had matured *by then* the villager couldn't say.

Whichever, the oaks had been rooted well into the Savernake soils for centuries because an oak does not produce acorns until it is at least 40 years old. As we strolled the paths I had to admit that the oaks were quite splendid and providing the only sound – that of hundreds of acorns showering to the ground in the continually rising wind.

I recall picking acorns from the paths of the deer-park at Wollaton close to my boyhood home. At the ages of eight or nine my friends and I regarded oaks and acorns as one tree type and its fruit. Not until we were older and perusing books on trees did we discover that there are several varieties of oak, each with its own hosting acorn type.

We had not, however, remained totally ignorant because there in the deer-park we gradually realised that we were looking at two types of acorn and, indeed, if we looked closely two types of leaves. Not surprisingly, then, we collectively absorbed the fact that in the average English oak-growing soils there were two types of oak.

The heavily crowned oaks, as I still think of them today, were, and still are – the recent decades of furious gales notwithstanding – English oaks. They bear heavy widespreading crowns borne on sometimes undulating branches, twisted yet, in winter, so significant against the winter sky. The leaves are lobed but, in deep patternings, irregular in shape – 'as to the leaf the shape of the tree'. But the acorns are the true giveaway signs due to them sitting neatly cupped on long stems. These, then, are the fruits of the *English* oak.

Competing for habitat, sustenance and space is the sessile oak. A decidedly slender-trunked tree, at first glance, with a less outspreading canopy. The sessile has another name 'durmast oak'. Its twigs are not prolific. Compared to the English oak the leaves of the sessile carry less pronounced lobes and the acorns are bereft of stalks. Perhaps because of its lack of woodiness, the sessile does not carry so many legends and, therefore, seems to feature less in folklore than the English oak. That said, both species were used for shipbuilding in the Elizabethan era and at an astonishing rate.

And thinking trees, I wonder how many small children today are taught that 'an oak spends 300 years growing, 300 years in its zenith and 300 years dying'!

The oaks are the hosting species to a variety of insects, weevils, moths, galls and gall wasps. Jays seek out their acorns and bury those that are regarded as surplus to their requirements. Tree creepers and nuthatches regard oak woods as priority habitats, along with the summering pied flycatchers.

Come the autumn, the oaks produce the most pungent of scents – as I have mentioned elsewhere – and here at Savernake, as light drizzle brings coatings of shiny baubles to the leaves, a world exists that, despite its dampness, produces much colour for the seasonal eye to revel in and the mind to take in the fact that every oak glade produces a unique world that will always remain unchallenged.

# OCTOBER

## The Barle Valley, Exmoor

A friend and I arrive at the ridge top farm just as the frosted dusk begins filtering in.

From a distance, in the valley beside the river, and with binoculars trained in the farm's direction, the house resembles little more than an isolated rock positioned on a ledge.

Yet, once one has travelled the long winding track across moorland, sheep pasture, and seen only the sky ahead, the farmhouse – nestled at the bottom of a steep hollow and best approached by vehicle in first gear – is rock sided, extensive and elongated like a building on the Scottish borders.

There are six or seven bedrooms, a dairy, kitchen, dining and guest rooms, two upstairs bathrooms, and stabling all ensconced within the same building.

The stockyard is built on the lower lip of the great ridge. Why did the farm's first inhabitants choose to live here? For the same reason surely that Neolithic Man and the later dwellers of Cresswell Crags chose to make permanent homes there – the proximity of clear, running water.

Springs erupt through the farmyard; clearwater that, strangely, we humans don't hear much by daylight but if we sleep with the windows open at midnight the songs of that precious water pleasantly and continually break through the blackened silence surrounding the buildings all around.

Fred Bawden, the farmer, allows six or seven cows to congregate in the forecourt stockyard during times of heavy snow. By doing that their tramplings and chafings prevent the snow from drifting and also from blocking the progress of the springs and streams.

In the memorabilia box within the house is a photograph of Fred with snow he's piled up by tractor reaching at least three quarters of the way up the yard's nearest telegraph pole.

Having given the cross-bred cattle dogs the backs of our hands to sniff before leaving the car and taking our gear into the house, we join Fred at the farm gate overlooking the valley.

On the walled field immediately below, a mature red deer stag stands centralised and, at intervals, roaring in a bid to let outlying hinds and followers know where his temporary stand is established. Not that he would have herded his small harem of hinds to that grassy slope as many choose to believe. The choice of a so-called rutting stand is made by the matriarch of the group, the oldest and, therefore, *leading* hind. The stag is the follower. When a herd of red deer move off, *under natural circumstances*, the hinds file off with the matriarch leading and the stag brings up the rear.

The stag's mane is mud-blackened due to constant wallows. His back is chestnut brown. He paces, muzzle uplifted, his nostrils reading the wind, head tilted slightly so that the backs of his antlers fall in line with his dorsal ridge. He paces and turns, runs swiftly to a hind that is couched and cudding. She rises, bounds away a few strides her small buff tail wagging. The stag lowers his head, sniffs the grass patch on which the hind was couched. He is checking her scent as to whether or not she is in oestrous. A red deer hind comes into oestrous for 24 hours every three weeks between the end of September and November. In small groups, such as are to be found on Exmoor and the Quantock Hills, a hind is usually served in her first term.

The stag below trots to the hind, his tongue flickering over his muzzle. She will not stand for him. Instead she trots away a further few steps. The stag roars. He turns towards the farm. Roars again. Turns towards Lychwell Wood, nestled in the valley on the other side of the Barle, and roars again. He is calling in more hinds.

If a hind *is* in oestrous there will be other stags in the vicinity awaiting a chance to cut her out. Mate with her should the opportunity arise.

I scan the valley with the naked eye. West of Lychwell Wood the land contours rise steeply and are bracken swathed. I check the bracken fronds for different autumnal colourations. Stag! Deep red coated. Couched and with his muzzle directed upon this hind group and the stag on the field before us. To his right a second stag. Tawny-coated by comparison but of equal antler spread and body size.

I point them out to Fred who is carrying binoculars. He is amazed because I picked both stags out from the bracken fronds with the naked eye.

"Why, Keith, you're obviously long-sighted! I've lived on Exmoor for every day of my 65 years and I've never picked out a stag at that distance!" he exclaims.

Fred locates them but through his binoculars. Mine, would I believe, are up in a farmhouse bedroom unpacked and sitting redundant on the bed. Nor can my friend locate those outlying stags with the naked eye.

Darkness dims the landscape gradually. The razor-sharp intensity of the incoming frost takes advantage of the dimming light. Frost increases the activity of the red deer rut, brings hinds into oestrous. Every Highland deerstalker will confirm that fact, but no one knows why.

In the farmhouse we eat and converse around the Aga until midnight with our hosts. In the bedroom, as if complete silence has attempted to well up to the height of the windows, the tinkling gush of the streams assure us of survival. So long as there is water…

At intervals the roars of the rutting stag carry across the blackened moor. Beneath the duvet I'm in a place of darkness, peace and seclusion. Where I want to be. Out there beyond the windows the night and its activities live on. It is only we humans who, because of the darkness, have fearfully withdrawn from the scene. At least, in my case, until daybreak.

## Nickel End, Derwent Water, Lake District

Sitting, backs to the trunk of a beech tree, binoculars in hand, as the russet curtains of leaf drift waft down and shred before our eyes.

Up there, look! On the long branch which provides a road and access to the branches on the next tree *red squirrel*. That is why we are here today. And up there is our quarry.

Searching, feeding, its prehensile body seems to be quivering from blunt round nose to tail tip. Follow it with your binoculars back along its highway, the beech branch to the trunk of that same beech. Ah, a second. Spread-eagled on the tree trunk waiting. A youngster I would say from here.

Notice how this one lacks ear tufts as yet and is a little more gingery on the coat. It's probably, what? Eight or nine weeks old by my reckoning but will rapidly develop the winter coat in the weeks, if not days, ahead.

Adult and youngster are spiralling in chase play around the tree trunk. Ah! Didn't see the second adult rummaging in the leaf litter at the foot of the tree. The first adult and the youngster are making their way down to it.

Red squirrels spend much less time on the ground than the grey. But the three, look, are now together while each parts a little from its kin to forage alone.

The youngster is probably a female or doe kept on the territory by the male or buck, in order to fulfil the role of a mate should he lose his original mate to a hawk or falcon. I suspect that all our little pockets of red squirrels must be inbred for there are not enough, *if indeed any*, occupying the periphery niches beyond the average breeding ground or sanctuary. The habitats may occasionally prove to be there, but there are still not enough red squirrels to occupy them.

*Play-chasing, look!* All three of them. Racing through the leaf carpets and whisking up and around the beech bole. God, they *can* move when they want to!

Look at the furling and unfurling of those long bushy tails. Jerking, describing every instinctive pulse – that of play at the moment – navigating the body. Their worlds, like those of most rodents and small related furry mammals, revolve around each other. They will sleep curled together in one of perhaps two or three moss-lined family dreys when the hard winds and driving snow shriek through these hills in a few months' time.

They will not, *do not*, hibernate because it is doubtful if either the grey or red squirrel can live much beyond four days without food. But they will sleep and, ultimately in that inner nest lined with mosses, conserve energy until hunger forces them out for another bout of feeding.

Down the tree bole now they come! Tail chasing. Scrabbling of claws. Eager it seems to return to the leaf litter. Those many colourful leaves layering the earth but on the ground surface being blown amongst and around the beech roots as if to preserve them. There are pine here, too, which is where, I suspect, one or more of the squirrel dreys will be lodged.

Chance for a binocular close-up. See that adult nibbling into a beech mast or fungi bracket 20 feet away?

Slow movements of the hands as you raise your binoculars, although its my guess that the squirrels know we are here. Probably saw us before we saw them.

So here in binocular close-up notice the whiskers quivering due to the motions of the jawline; the almost liquid clear eye; rounded muzzle and pronounced ear tufts, indicating that the adults are already in winter coat.

The fur of the body looks instantly strokeable, the tail jerking as if in anticipation of the squirrel's next move and almost like a red antennae attached directly to the small inner workings of its brain.

The tail and ear tufts provide an endearing study for us humans. Had the red squirrel, or the fox come to that, a hairless tail we would find both mammals far less attractive. Especially the fox with its narrow pointed muzzle and pricked ears.

Notice, through your binoculars, how each squirrel bites without hesitation into its selected nut or kernel. Mature squirrels especially know exactly where to bite to crack the shell or skin of each food item. Look how those two before us move a nut so swiftly into position before taking their first gnawing bite. Their forepaws are the equivalent of human hands and the squirrel's read the shape of each nut or kernel in order to gain immediate entry.

The younger squirrel out there? Well, he or she is still experimenting. Still learning to *read* a nutshell. But it will not be fumbling and false biting for long. Nature doesn't allow for that. The teeth of a squirrel are like pincered chisels and a mature squirrel is able to crack the average nut or kernel apart with one bite. It not only knows exactly where to hold it but also which position to use in respect of those teeth. The lower jaw, in particular, comes into play and it is the incisors that must surely split the casing into half.

As boys, collecting acorns in our close-to-home deer-park, we usually discovered that the squirrel which had discarded one had begun by making a small incisor groove at the pointed end. You might see this now *today* through your binoculars. If so, notice, as the squirrel sits with the acorn clasped in its furry forepaws, how the lower incisor actually does the shell slitting while the upper incisor acts as a grip. True, you need powerful binoculars to detect such actions but at the Formby Red Squirrel Reserve in Lancashire – although not immediately discernible to the naked human eye – such dexterity can be observed at relatively close quarters.

Back to those early days clambering around the roots of the deer-park oaks, we youngsters also found acorns that were half split, or with shells chipped and bruised. We then surmised, perhaps rightly in some instances, that a pheasant or jay had made unsuccessful attempts to pierce those acorns and make those marks. But, in retrospect, it was probably the young red squirrels of the year that were responsible and still experimenting, so late in the season, as to how to extract the pithy food contents with the minimum of effort.

Green, yellow and russet leaves. The red question mark shapes of three feeding red squirrels. Blue sky with white cumulus. Leaves drifting… drifting from the last deciduous tree en route to John o' Groats to the last en route to Land's End. Leaves brushing our jacket shoulders as we sit, a leaf or two settling in our hair or on our cloth caps.

Before, binoculars in hand, we steal away just smell the musk, *the woodiness* so characteristic of the Welsh and English woodland tracts since deciduous trees were planted, either by man or the natural cycle, and matured to provide food for our small bird and mammal species, although we shouldn't overlook the deer which are also attracted to the ground layer acorns, beech mast and sweet-chestnuts.

We make our way back to the green-mossed walls, the damp moss and cracks within them adhered with fallen leaves and spider webs. Here, as in every thicketed nook and cranny, the robins reel out their autumn songs.

But let us now move on. Disturb nothing.

## North Yorkshire

Travelling south early morning over the Yorkshire Moors. Woods hazed in an occasional distance. The open roads snaking over and around massive ground contours intersecting landscapes of glorious heather.

I am surprised because there are still curlews up here, calling. Long-beaked waders with pale underwings, which they flap conspicuously in order that others of their species can locate them.

Are these, still in these uplands, getting ready for their migrational flights to our estuaries, sewage farms and gravel-extraction lakes well south of here? Are they ready to assemble, those remaining birds that enhance the skylines and stalk over the heather tufts, alert, almost querulous.

From a car lay-by we study them. Their evolved elegance. But balanced so strategically and fitting into the landscape and with none of the barely credible ugliness of flamingoes.

The bill of the curlew is long, slender and distinctive when seen in silhouette. The bill is 'D' curved. The mottled black, fawnish, inner browns of the crop and paleness of the underparts differ slightly between the summer and winter feathers.

One of a pair that a local lad once had the temerity to ask me to identify, had a pinkish tinge on the lower mandible while the second did not. The lad wasn't even aware that he had shot curlew. 'Two things moved' on the local marshes-cum-rubbish tip so he shot them.

There are variants, but slight, in young and adult plumage patterns but only a scientist bent on a study to do with wader conservation needs really to know those.

The experts insist that the female curlew is larger than the male and that they leave the brood at the end of June or into early July and fly to the estuaries, thus embarking on journeys of partial migration. The leggy youngsters are then watched over by the brood male. But why this form of avian seasonal arrangement exists I, nor anyone with whom I have touched upon the subject, could say. It may have to do with the fact that the female of some wader species, having lost perhaps some weight and body fuel during their period of incubation and the ultimate egg chippings, need to move away, not only to moult but rejuvenate. Get back into condition. Hence their arrival at the estuaries and sewage farms early.

The 'cur-lee' call of the curlews was one of the first sound recordings played by the BBC to us wartime children sitting wide-eyed and, in my case, already peppered by wanderlust, in those classrooms in which each desk had daily to be checked to ensure that gas masks glared ominously up at us when the lid was lifted.

The normally four blotched eggs are vulnerable to moorland fox predation if the female is taken from the nest or happens to be away feeding.

Foxes are mobbed by long-billed waders like godwits and whimbrel but often to no avail. Egg between its jaws or not, the fox keeps trotting until it is clear of their breeding range.

Returning, then, to the curlew population still frequenting the autumn moors. Are the majority of these the males and near adult young that have still to leave? From what the experts tell me it would appear so.

Leaving the high contours we drive down into and through the Dales. And, so far as the village greens and thatched cottages are concerned, can Wensleydale be bettered?

At Bainbridge we pull in for coffee. Here we learn that the 'classic Yorkshire Inn' houses the horn of an ox. This horn was blown – *and is still today* – to guide the fourteenth-century foresters home in the times when the Dales were tracts of great forest.

The inn, I should add, is the Rose and Crown, the only public house in Bainbridge and which dates back to the year 1445. It is, not surprisingly, listed as being one of the oldest inns in Yorkshire.

The horn is sounded still from 27 September (Holy Rood) until Shrove Tuesday in the period of long, often overcast, autumn and winter days.

And speaking of tradition, the old village stocks are to be seen here out on the broad village greens. No two Dale villages seem exactly the same. There are village stocks, village greens and roadside creameries, yet the character, *the feel*, of each differs slightly.

There are glimpses and, indeed, stopping places where the River Ure runs a bejewelled gauntlet throughout this extensive National Park.

In the haw thickets bordering Aysgarth Falls the robins are singing and will be singing from every other haw or blackthorn thicket between here, home and beyond.

That sense of something missing on every journey now reminds us that the swallows and house martins have journeyed to the Mediterranean countries and will be journeying beyond in due course. The telegraph wires are bereft of them and will remain so while the future threats of snowstorms creep imperceptibly across the autumnscapes and into the winter scene.

As for ourselves, our journey is homeward; south on routes potentially more lethal today than those taken by the migrating birds.

## Morley, Derbyshire

The woods around here - and not so distant Shipley - persuade us to hunt for the fungi species which come to fruition now.

Damp, deciduous woodland tracts, stands of silver birch and bracken, hiding such gems as the poisonous fly agaric, all play their part in attracting the naturalists - and *hopefully* many *young* naturalists in for a foray or two.

These woods are not unique but typical of those to be found in many an English county. Every natural habitat harbours types of fungi which intersperse with rotting timber, leaf mould ditch sides. Trees also nurture their fungi types - rotting stumps and branches.

Wherever they are to be found they have, or are the result of, released spores. Of, if we prefer to think of them as such, *seeds*. Tiny mites - of which we humans know or care little - must eat these in quantity. Under normal circumstances we cannot see the mites and so erase them from our minds, if ever they were there in the first place.

The spores which survive, however, create yet another harvest. That of the fungi type which is related to them.

We are best acquainted with the fruiting bodies which, on fungi forays, can be located when involved in the enjoyable task of sifting through wooded and mossy nooks and crannies. Or carefully uncovering layers of leaves. Absorbing the nutrients for each fruiting body is a main stem or 'hyphae' which preys on the cambium layer of trees, within dead leaves, on tree stumps and root clusters which have been left in the ground.

Different types of fungi have different ways of dispersing their spores. Fungi spores can lay low for a time until conditions persuade them to develop, and as the hyphae become widespread they form a fruiting carpet known as a mycelium and, as fungi hunters, that is what we are seeking or are looking at.

The autumn, then, is the best time to be fungi hunting but, although I look for and occasionally photograph fungi types, I am never persuaded to eat them. Food from the woodland floor, so be it. But not for me. Particularly on seeing the sickly state of a friend who breakfasted on fried shaggy inkcaps! He was off work with an upset stomach for three days.

Mycelium below the ground layers survives for years. But as the frosts set in and bring more leaves from the trees – at an accelerated rate – the fungi species die off. Signs of nibbling woodmice and squirrels are found around toadstools. Snails and slugs are not adverse to certain types and deer pluck off the caps and swallow them accordingly. They may briefly chew fungi before swallowing but the processes of nibbling are left to the small mammals and insects.

# NOVEMBER

## Wollaton, Nr Nottingham

Nostalgic for the aromatic tangs of woodsmoke, I go an hour before dusk up to a local wood and share a fire with the itinerant.

Stooped, bearded and in his late forties, Joe welcomes me and was aware of someone approaching when the blackbirds, and far fewer jays, gave out their warnings as I wended up the bracken slope.

Woodsmoke, Joe's twinkling-eyed welcome and a felled beech log to sit on while we talk and watch the flames. Could a man ask for more?

He had left the wood earlier, gone to the shops and bought the bacon slices and a portion of black pudding which he has on the frying pan he holds over the flames. He doesn't eat fungi. 'Not naturalised enough' as he puts it. Besides which he cannot positively identify all the species because, due to his own admitted unkempt appearance, he is quickly turned out of the libraries which he sometimes goes into in attempts to sift through the natural history books and field guides.

Joe is eccentric to the point of these days always wearing the same long overcoat. He prefers to sleep in deep rhododendron covert, the majority of which was planted – along with bamboo – in the eighteenth century to provide shelter for the gentry's pheasants.

His mattress is usually the earth itself, lined with fallen oak leaves. Covered by an old canvas-type sheet he sleeps with the scents of the season's bluebells in May, leaf mould and the associated driftings in October and November. But should the chill of winter become so severe that he feels his 'innards might freeze' he leaves the woods to spend a night or two at an old flat in an equally old part of the city.

As Joe brings a loaf of sliced bread into the scene and tests the contents of the frying pan, I study his profile then tell him quite openly that he is probably the nearest Homo sapien to Cresswell Crags Man that I will probably meet throughout the rest of my lifetime.

Chuckling as he puts his frying-pan-finalised sandwiches together, Joe admits that he would like to make the 40-mile journey to Cresswell and live in one of the caves. But, of course, the 'authorities' would turn him out.

Above and around us now the dusk resounds with the excited chatter of blackbirds. Joe hears it every winter's dusk. Myself, only if I go out to listen for it.

The blackbirds are extremely vocal and will remain so while the tawny owls are tentatively leaving their roosts for the hours of darkness ahead in which they will hunt and feed. And as the tawny owls waft, dome-headed, through the tree branches so the blackbirds attempt to mob them and loudly warn other blackbirds, probably the young of the year, that predators are on the prowl.

'Picka picka picka. Picka picka' the blackbirds are on leaf sprays, tree branches and literally running the gauntlet of the elongated branches of oak, beech and silver birch. Their wings are flicking, their tails jerking as if motivated by clockwork.

Such avian pandemoniums occur in every tract of deciduous woodland throughout Britain in these darkening days of late autumn and on through the winter. Not that the blackbirds have little cause for concern for they feature on the tawny owl's menu – both at dusk and daybreak – when they return to their natal woods for roosting.

A late friend, seeing the shine of metal calling him over as he walked a local leaf mould glade, discovered the pellet discarded by a tawny owl within which, shaped like a tiny concertina, was the British Trust of Ornithology ring that had been fitted by bird ringers on the leg of a mist netted blackbird.

In having caught and devoured the blackbird the tawny owl had also swallowed the aluminium ring, and the concertina shape indicated just how strong were the workings of its gizzard as it transformed the ring accordingly. The ring was, of course, numbered and my friend sent it to the British Trust of Ornithology. In due time he received word that the blackbird had been netted in that same tract of woodland nine years earlier.

Joe keeps as clean as he can. Along with his frying pan he keeps rolls of toilet paper and kitchen towels in the hollow of a tree.

Twice a week – summer and winter alike – he swims in the clay pools, now discarded by a firm of plant pot makers, edging onto a wood three miles from here. His towels, after hanging them on tree branches to dry out, he stows in another tree hollow.

He journeys, then, from wood to wood. Living with and, in winter, sometimes *against* nature as best he can.

At his flat he will bath properly, trim his hair and beard. But the weather has to be severe in order for him to be making his way there. He has a little money put by and claims nothing from the state.

But what motivated him into choosing this way of life? I ask.

Joe needed a challenge. Something more than the working week schedule. He felt the need to pit his wits against an unseen force. Consequently, and perhaps not surprisingly, he chose the elements. Yet he loved life so much that he persuaded himself not to gamble his life away due to this unyielding challenge.

As a youngster he would have stirred the sexual yearnings in not a few women. That is my admission, not *his*. Even now he unwittingly carries the aura of a Spanish conquistador. Unkempt, ageing. But weathering well.

On leaving school he took a job as a folder in a lace factory situated in the heart of our natal city. In his spare hours he played football and, like myself, looked for the suburban equivalents to wildernesses in which to wander. But he loathed what he calls 'the plottings of women'. And the lace trade employed good numbers of them.

He detested, as I do myself, 'tittle-tattle'. Underhanded victimisations caused largely, he and I believe, through occupational boredom.

Came the day when Joe himself became the victim of such plottings. He was ambushed, seized, de-bagged and stripped naked by a crowd of lace trade employees. All women, hooting and screaming with laughter.

Angered and embarrassed, he dressed, walked out of the premises and never returned to the lace trade again.

Instead he became a collier, a coal miner. He would receive better working with men, he concluded. He would not be abused. Nor was he. Miners, like everyone, Joe and I included, had their shortcomings. But beneath the ground, inside the corridors of the earth, they all nurtured the same respect for survival. When they – at the beginning of each shift – descended in the cage, each of them secretly wondered if they would see daylight again. Twenty years on and the feeling never left Joe. And probably not his colleagues, we agreed.

He marvelled at the great sheets, the great walls of coal, the remnants of petrified forests, providing foundational bases for the world above and about which no person above ever thought about or considered the existence of. There were shafts, *streets* hewn from coal by generations of miners who had gone before him.

Joe appreciated all this but in his mid-forties the *need for the challenge* gnawed at his mind. And repeatedly. It was time, his mind and body told him, to come above ground, permanently. And so he turned to the woods which is where, brooding over a winter fire, I first met him.

He always mentions the sheer joy he experiences when awakening in a morning with his beard soaked in dew. Quite a few times he has opened his eyes to see a robin peering in at him. Or was startled suddenly by grey squirrels running over his back and shoulders.

Music? He is surrounded by birdsong in the summer and the refrains of robins throughout the darker months.

He learns from the wood pigeons with regards to people coming up to the wood. And that is when he hides his possessions in the hollow tree and makes himself scarce.

On a morning just previous to my visit he had put a shop packet containing a portion of black pudding at his booted heels as he prepared the fire and frying pan, then turned at a sudden flurry as a fox bounded off with the black pudding pack in its jaws.

Living? Joe has certainly done that. And close to the natural world, *within* the natural world. Which is why I need to occasionally seek him out for, like most of his kind, he usually has a tale to tell.

## Hyde Park, London

Near on midday and I'm strolling by the Serpentine. The water surface shimmers with long slanting streamers of golden light.

Having completed their moult, the swan pair with nine cygnets sail like an arch-winged Armada along the water's edge. Skewbald now, the cob cygnets are the size of their male parent. The entire family are immaculately preened and oiled. But it is not the daily supply of visitors' bread alone that has helped them develop. It is the instinctive workings of the pen's mind because cygnets need to feed on some form of greenery – preferably water plants – and on the lakes of the Royal Parks – due to boating and an overpopulation of wildfowl – these are not abundant. Therefore, the family fed on a rich substitute – grass.

This particular cob and pen, when the cygnets are around a month old, lead them daily across the parkland's grassy slopes to The Round Pond in Kensington Gardens. En route, and not infrequently harassed by unleashed dogs, the family grazes, taking in quantities of grass, particularly following overnight rain.

In recent years some twenty or thirty non-breeding, or *pre-breeding*, swans have congregated on the same water and grazed the grasslands around Kensington Palace. Again these grasslands are their localised equivalents of water meadows.

The cob swan of this breeding pair is an exceptionally large bird. Consequently, the majority of his male protégé now equal him in size and will hold prominent positions in the mute swan societies of the future.

Thinking thus, I become aware of an old Asian gentleman coming to the water's edge with a carrier bag filled with bread slices, as many people do. Wearing a woollen hat, bearded and well wrapped, he throws quantities of bread out to the swan family and other waterfowl but breaks pieces up with his fingers for the smaller birds; the passerines.

Twenty or so starlings fly in. They position themselves between my shoe tips and the old Asian who nonchalantly tosses a tiny bread morsel to a grounded starling which catches the morsel in its beak and swallows accordingly. These motions are repeated. And again. The starling is so well coordinated with the old Asian's aim that it never misses. Each tossed morsel goes straight down its open gullet. Nine… ten… fourteen times. There is no squabbling with the other starlings because man and bird are working together. They are an act. And that act, I decide, is performed daily at around this time.

This tells me something else – that this particular starling is a local bird. And so probably are its feathered peers. I am intrigued and wishing I had a movie camera at my disposal. There must be bird- and animal-feeding humans who have relationships with different birds and mammals throughout London. The grey squirrel enthusiasts are to be seen every day. But there are other feeding relationships abounding, of that I feel certain.

I recall now the late October afternoon when, en route and walking from the office of a London publisher to St Pancreas, I sat on a bench by the arm of the lake in Regent's Park. Immediately I relaxed, a cluster of house sparrows flew in. Instead of settling at my feet they fluttered to the back of the bench, or hopped onto my shoulders, or nuthatch-like inspected my elbows and coat for that single dropped crumb which I hadn't produced.

'Another scarecrow here, look! Has it brought any bread or cakes or birdseed with it?'

In truth I didn't have a morsel to offer these delightful little birds. But they flew to my knees, lap and shoulders nevertheless.

The cock birds displayed fanned tails when a hen bird came close, the hen birds leading them on – bonding-wise – with their 'chip chip cheep' acknowledgements.

The cart-pulling horses with their nosebags of grain are 60 years removed from our city streets. There is no grain in the gutters for the house sparrows to feed on and many old buildings, which provided nesting niches – 'colonies' in some instances – have been demolished. There is less food. Consequently, there are far fewer house sparrows. But our farms, holdings and well-established garden centres now provide habitat *and* with weatherproofed roosting conditions. Such establishments are the saviours of our house sparrows in this, the twenty-first, century.

Fortunately, the London parks still nurture a few colonies and certain paths in Regent's Park make no secret of the fact.

One of the sparrows on my seat that late afternoon I managed to tickle gently at the back of its nape. And probably, as far as the bird was concerned, not for the first time. The colouration here is unique – chocolatey russet. The brown and black streaks make me, yet again, aware of the powers of evolution. The singular cluster of cells and all that stems through and within them to create each species. *Incredible.*

The crown of the male house sparrow is blueish grey; the cheeks are whitish grey; and a black patch surrounds the eye, extends down the throat and spreads to the upper crop, below which dingy white covers its underparts. They appear to be stiff-tailed, but in throaty musical courtship male or cock sparrows spread the tail upwards and outwards like a miniature male domesticated turkey.

Way back in the sixties on one of our visits to London Zoo, my wife Jean and I, with our children, made for the cage-cum-enclosure holding the anthropoid bulk of the legendary gorilla, Guy. Guy was aware of us but unimpressed. As the children mentioned later 'he just sat looking'.

Moving on and around Guy's quarters, just a little ahead of the family, I paused to look at the Rhesus monkeys and was silenced by the fact that the local intake of baby house sparrows were flitting through the secondary mesh wiring of the monkeys' extensive cage and perched on the branches within. In one swift movement each monkey grabbed the nearest baby house sparrow, bit off its head, chewed for seconds only then spat the beak and skull onto the gravelled floor of the enclosure. At that time of year the zookeeper must have been sweeping decapitated house sparrows up every day, I reflected. In retrospect, I have sometimes wondered if that is what the children – and other visiting children – ought to have been seeing. As it was I decided to leave the situation while still aware of the fact that these predations would have been taking place in the Rhesus monkeys' natural habitat anyway.

## Dumfrieshire, Scotland

Leaving the wildfowl reserve at Caeverloch Castle, we voiced our disappointment because the annually visiting skeins of barnacle geese had not, by then, arrived.

"No more than a dozen a day at the moment. And they aren't staying for any length of time," the warden assured us.

In a village adjacent to the converted railway worker's cottage where we stayed for several nights, the post office clerks working behind the counter grill enthused on the fact that golden eagles could be seen daily, through the post office windows. But, again, not a single eagle appeared for us.

The remote and winding Dumfrieshire roads, however, were colourful, and the mosses adorning the drystone walls and decorated by russet leaves interwoven with spider webs I couldn't resist photographing.

The woods here flowed with the pungent scents of the autumn as any in England. Robins twined. Threads of gossamer drifted, backlit when tree foliage gaps allowed, yet rode on air currents that neither our eyes or a wetted fingertip could detect.

On moors, hemmed in by forestry blocks of commercial pine, we meditated in long heathery grasses while scanning the silvered surface of both Loch Ken and Loch Skerrow. Only the split silvered water trail made by an otter would break an hour or so of meditation, we agreed. By each sunset we had seen nothing resembling these intriguing water sprites that also travel overland.

The Dee, yodelling in places by islets of rock, suggested our route homeward. Follow its song and you will arrive at the cottage. There was no fog; a hint of frost and nothing more.

Eventually the sunset became distorted as seemingly endless skeins of whickering pink-footed geese crossed in V formations, flying in and over from the sea to feed on the flatlands surrounding the lochs we had vacated.

With the darkness homing in, they would roost in a great split concourse on each surface of those two lochs. Bill tips tucked into scapulars, one paddle dangling beneath the depths to provide secure anchorage.

When the geese were down silence reigned, and I, if not my companions, bathed my mind in it. Each evening I gave my brain a mental sauna, after which I eagerly closed the cottage door and faced the flame patterns and charred resin scents emanating from the pine log fire.

Nor did we leave the cottage until each following daybreak.

## Park Hall, Staffordshire

Teeming rain. Great swathes of slanting ice water dominating the drive south-west to this designated country park area, comprising largely Forestry Commission pine hiding a sequence of quarries, both shallow and deep.

Had I gone there with the prospects of a day's exploration in mind, I would have been disappointed, especially in fair weather. The landscape is broken –

ravaged by human industrialised intervention – but planted with relatively fast growing evergreen trees, varied pines, in the manner of using a swiftly acquired tablecloth in a bid to hide the scratches on the surface of an antiquarian table. On a day of bitter weather I may have viewed it differently.

The journey took an hour in ceaseless rain. However, wet and icy though the morning was proving to be, warmth and enthusiasm swarmed in as our host and guide, Pete, the local countryside ranger, welcomed us inside the otherwise deserted visitors' centre. We dried gear on the backs of chairs and Pete soon had mugs of hot tea proffered into the cradling palms of our hands.

Countryside ranging. I know from experience, can be a lonely occupation during spells of inclement weather. Pete had been on bird watching trips to India and Gambia and lost no time in colouring us in on his forays.

The quarries of this country recreation area hosted chiefly stonechats and little owls. But we were there to hopefully gain binocular close-ups of two long-eared owls which roosted on the edge of a pine tract a few yards from the centre.

Half an hour later, and reclad in waterproofs and boots, we followed Pete out into the tempest. Rain thudded against our hoods and thornproofs. There was no romanticism, no song of pattering. The raindrops *thudded*; crashed into our slightly cowering, near upright, frames; attempted to penetrate our boots and clothing but was unsuccessful, although when rain did briefly chance upon a narrowed section of our cheeks it proved to be damn-near-freezing rain.

In a glade amongst the pines Pete halted and pointed upwards. Thirty feet above, and obviously damp of plumage but relatively sheltered by the shelvings of evergreens, perched the two long-eared owls. One was positioned upright but with slitted eyes as if dozing. The second stared down at us.

Binocular focus soon had those orange-rimmed eyes in view, with the socket recesses, as one may refer to them, a warm, downy orange. Both owls, their 'ears' held upright and the white frontal bars between the eye sockets and the curved bill partially covered with down, were conspicuous in the damp, green-tinged, forest gloom. Below the facial discs of these vole-dependent predators, the body – feather-wise – is streaked with black on an inner feather toning of fawnish grey. Good light is needed to really appreciate the varied tones of a long-eared owl. And such light should reveal the beadings of white, though not frequent, contrasting with the darker plumage which also carries its variations.

Beneath an owl's roost the pellets, or digested remains of the bird's food sources, are to be found. The pellets vary according to the species. I well remember sheltering from a shower in a small tractor shed positioned by a field track and finding the tractor seat pretty well covered with the black leathery pellets ejected by the barn owls roosting on a beam above. Knowing countrymen look for pellets beneath the tree roosts known to be frequented by owls, although tawny owls in particular are notorious roost changers, *within their chosen territories*, and, not surprisingly, will favour evergreen roosts during the autumn and winter months.

A scattering of pellets beneath the pines would have given the Park Hall long-eared owls away. But a ranger or volunteer has to be vigilant and searching for them in the first place. There must also be a supply of voles, other small mammals and birds within the habitat – or hunting zone – of an owl or most avian predator species.

By then, selecting our route because the outer forest paths were becoming waterlogged, we were satisfied and sloshed back to the visitor centre.

Shaking hands with and thanking Pete, we then set off for an hour's journey to the north-east and home.

As we travelled so a westerly wind rose and moved the clouds. Diffused sunlight made an appearance.

With yet another mug of tea, I sat dry in the flat and looking out onto the soaking thickets beyond the windows. In my absence leaves had been torn from the branches of my beloved silver birches at seemingly an alarming rate.

Peace, interspersed with stronger rays of sunlight however, created a soothing atmosphere inside the rooms. There was no need to talk, just sit with tea and imbibe the peace. Think back to the forest glade and the rain – which seemed now connected to another morning, *another world* – and Pete's gift of a pair of long-eared owls which we didn't even have to unwrap.

# DECEMBER

## Wollaton, Near Nottingham

Although I had the right, I turned an unaccustomed blind eye to the woman with secateurs who was snipping off holly branch strands from a tree on the wood's edge, and chose not to reprimand her. It is the holly berry season, after all. When she saw me approaching in the Land Rover, an expression of guilt replaced her earlier expression of delight in wanting her home to portray all the elements of Christmas. I drove slowly by and she and I exchanged 'good mornings'. That was it. I'd much rather the occasional person snip a holly swathe from a tree than be roaming with an uncontrollable dog off the lead and the potential hazards of there being deer feeding or resting in the glades beyond.

Never once would I ignore a person with a dog loose and walking in the vicinity of livestock, whether the livestock was mine or my employer's. But, by contrast, to have holly around the rooms in these fast approaching days of the winter solstice is a warming thought. Like most people I tend to only see an importance in holly in December. The definitive picture lodges in my mind, whereas holly – like much else – has been naturally propagating towards a decent harvest, much like every plant, crop, moss and fungi substance.

Holly belongs to the group of plants which stay green throughout the winter. Despite the chills it continues to grow and store nutrients. In other words it continues photosynthesising. Thus, when the leaves have fallen from the deciduous trees towering above it, the holly takes advantage of the light, and the water – rain and snow of course – and prospers accordingly.

Most, if not all, evergreen plants – such as holly – contain a natural flow of what could best be described as 'anti-freeze' within their sap canals, plus an exterior layer of natural wax which serves as weatherproofing. To the human touch the leaves appear hard, leathery. But holly on the underside appears comparatively dull to the human eye for within the leaf surfaces are minute needle-type pricks – best seen through a microscope – and these enable the holly to breathe.

Holly trees are either male or female, and, as with mistletoe, it is the female which bears the berries. At the age of around four years a holly tree may be seen to shed old leaves, but it will not be left bereft of new growth by any stretch of the imagination.

The cycle is slow. There is no sap rush to meet the increasing warmth and light, both of which the holly barely recognises. Consequently, there is no 'harvest rush'. 'All in good time' is the holly's message and there's not an entity on this planet that can force it to do otherwise.

Back in the sixties countryman Ted Ellis, writing in his national newspaper column, suggested that all berries were coloured to attract birds in to feed. He was not wrong. Holly, along with Rowan berries, is sought after by all members of the thrush family – residents or winter visiting – and starlings, whose visiting likenesses – waxwings – also seek them out.

In most tracts of commercially forested pine, miniature holly trees can be seen rising up through the needles and struggling to regenerate. Such sign indicates that the pines above them were used as winter roosts by fieldfares, redwings, blackbirds, starlings, possibly waxwings and a ring ousel or two; the droppings of which contained seedings that quickly found anchorage in the pine-acidic soils and set about their regenerative cycles.

Although we all think of them as being berries, fruits – such as the sloe, elder, wild cherry and holly – are scientifically monitored as drupes. This term signifies that each nodule of fruit contains a stone which encases a tiny, soft *but progressive*, seed. Nevertheless, I feel that the line of the carol in which 'the holly bears a berry' is apt and, of course, folklorist. I wouldn't want it changed for the word 'drupe'.

Each morning when I dissect the hay bales and strew the hay out over the grass, along with the swedes and mangolds with which to feed the park deer, I revel in the smell of those bales. Encased within them are the warm, sunlit and scented, smells of the previous summer. And so welcoming on daybreaks which hurl sleet across the parklands to the extent of the iced particles being heard patterning on my thornproofs.

The harder the weather the more deer assemble on the feeding area, as opposed to sheltering in the woods, which many of them return to once they have sated their respective hungers for turnips, swedes and hay. The stags of most age groups remain – couched, cudding or, alternatively, grass-grazing – until the next feeding trailer appears an hour before dusk.

The mature beasts often gather snow or sleet layers on the insides of their antlers. And a very definite pecking order exists with the stags literally 'horning in' if their herd peers display a reluctance to move aside for them.

By the winter – and due to the autumn rut – every stag in the herd is aware of the aggression, *or not*, of its neighbour. The same can be said for the fallow bucks which, again, recognise each other as individuals within the cervine gatherings.

Fallow does and their family followers will surge in amongst the bucks of their species and the red deer. But in some deer-park herds either the stags or the hinds show a reluctance to mix to any noticeable degree. There is, or seems to be, a definitive gender line. Some mixing *does* occur, but not regularly. In one deer-park, for instance, the *main* hind herd stays away from the stags and winter-feeding fallow deer. In another it is the stags which stay away, but feed if a tractor and trailer is taken out to their herding area. It is possible that, where a gender grouping is not mixing during the day, they come in to feed during the night, since deer are basically nocturnal feeders.

Distributing mangolds and swedes and splitting them

in halves so that the deer can bite into their sugary but starch-type inners, I love to watch the gait of the animals as they mill around. The 18-month-old males, carrying their first uprights and known by the medieval term of 'prickets' in England but 'staggies' in Scotland, stay clear of the antlers carried by senior beasts but eject hinds and calves from the swedes and beet by lowering the uprights and using them as threats. The three- to six-year-old stags trot beautifully between individuals of the herd, their heads raised and forelegs describing a mincing, sometimes trotting, gait which suggests that they are on the balls of their hooves. In this manner they resemble the colts and foals of thoroughbred horses and appear so flexible in body and ribcage structure. This flexibility enables them to turn or swerve aside with a grace and beauty that holds the seasonal eye spellbound in the seconds that such movements are being executed.

These younger stags also carry an awareness of the dominance and aggression, *or not*, that can be potentially exhibited by their rivals. The older stags – which can be carrying 230lbs of venison within their thickening frames – are slightly less agile. Nevertheless, they are swift and springy movers, especially when, on the winter feeding areas, they find themselves alongside a potential or recognised rival.

The older stags also vary in body shape, like the maturing bodies of most life forms, including us humans. They become decidedly saddle-backed as they approach their tenth season and, in some cases, an observer could be right in thinking the stags were bearing arthritic limbs. Nevertheless, between the ages of nine and eleven, assuming that the ground provides enough calcium and mineral deposit, including copper, a red deer stag can be seen carrying his finest head of antlers.

As with all living things, the skull shape changes as a deer reaches maturity. The jawline becomes elongated. Even the skull shapes of us humans change, ask any pathologist or portrait painter. With deer, the changing shape of each individual aids the stalker or controller in taking out what he or she thinks should be taken out of each age grouping.

Deer need to be culled to keep numbers to an even, *balanced*, ratio. Stags and bucks hereabout are usually culled in September, before the meat turns rancid due to the sexual chemistries of the autumn rutting season, and hinds and followers in the winter months, particularly December. There are no chases, in the old-fashioned sense. And very little spilt blood. But 525 deer cannot be kept on 525 acres of enclosed ground, simply because they won't have the food to sustain them. And this is the problem with all our deer-parks, many of which today seem grossly overstocked anyway.

In a wild state – and thousands of years ago – the wolf, wolverine, puma, lynx and bear reduced the populations of the deer herds. They took out the injured, the sick and the elderly. Now that we maintain deer herds in parks and in tracts of forest country or across moorland, they have no natural predators. Consequently, mankind has to play a role.

My own grazing programme – if I were in a sole position of deer management – would be to graze one deer to six acres of ground. That way I would expect to maintain healthy specimens. Many deer managers, who claim that their estates are blessed with 'lush grazings' and which may well be the case, prefer a one-deer-to-three-acres-type policy.

When members of the public show concern over these annual culls, which, one way or another, have been taking place since 1086 and probably before, I explain that, as Homo sapiens, we, too, have our natural predators – cancer and heart disease. These dreaded diseases may not stalk us in one sense, but they do in another. We are 'managed' and Nature takes its toll.

In the days of the great country houses, the staff of those estates nurturing deer were given venison portions and haunches at Christmas time, along with holly wreaths and evergreen boughs. No payments were accepted and obviously the ever poor village folk were truly grateful. As for the servant staff, they were usually awarded venison with their meals but seldom, if ever, allowed to return to their family homes at Christmas-tide.

A maid of any rank, shoeshine boy, groom or ostler, if not residing in the village, was allowed home for one week every six months. However, the *parents* of each domestic servant prospered because the families of all members of the lower class staff were sent, by post – meaning carrier cart – and by rail, hampers to their homes. And these hampers contained bottles of wine, nectarines, bananas and peaches grown in the hothouses of the great manor house, usually a waxed posy of camellias, gardenias or water lilies, and a haunch of venison, along with the customary greetings card. All for free.

Putting out hay, straw and turnips, then, on these

sleet-inclined mornings reminds me of those forgotten times and long forgotten people.

And beyond the sleet squalls the deer are still milling around for food – reason enough for anyone to be standing out in whatever weather just to marvel at the evolved beauty of these splendid animals.

## Lincolnshire Wolds

A card and letter from friends of long standing informed me that, due to chronic arthritis, they are leaving their Lincolnshire turkey farm and moving – on medical advice – to a warmer climate. To Spain, in fact.

The farming of turkeys – on a commercial scale – is no easy task since from time to time, and perhaps more often than is realised, turkeys need to be manhandled, and they are no lightweights.

I was first aware of turkeys nesting in a wild state when I was a boy. One of my many books on wildlife featured a pair of American Brush turkeys at their nest. The nest, a mound of vegetation, was every inch as big as that made by a pair of mute swans.

Brush turkeys served as food sources for the Native American tribes and the early white settlers, along with bison, deer and antelope. Those Brush turkeys were darkly plumaged and so were the farmyard turkeys that I glimpsed on passing in wartime. It is believed that their lineage in this country and Europe is due to transportation by the sixteenth-century explorers of the New World.

Whether, after that time, the turkeys were released into the wild lowlands of Britain or farmed is difficult to define. But one thing is certain. They were not raised in buildings resembling aircraft hangars and mass produced while expecting to live little more than 12 weeks as they are in present times. Nor was their plumage white.

The original introduced turkey breeds in this country were known as Spanish Blacks. Once they were established in Norfolk the name was changed to Norfolk Blacks. The Norfolk Black remained the unchallenged breed for 200 or 300 years. However, my friends in the business now enthuse upon the Bronze, so named because of the feathering tints. It is a slightly weightier bird with a larger crop or breast and is mostly reared as a free-range bird. Of the two breeds the Norfolk Black is deemed to be the tastier, turkey being a dry meat. But the Black retains its moisture and, therefore, to some considerable extent, its flavour. That said, both breeds sell well as table birds and are reared by enthusiasts who ensure that the majority roam free range, or as close to it as can be made possible.

The average turkey from these breeds lives for 24–27 weeks until it reaches its weight for slaughter. They are deemed to taste good because their growing period enables them to wax good meat. It is not unusual for a turkey to have been hung for a week after slaughter.

The majority are hand plucked, which, again, is no easy task, even for a singular turkey, due to the fact that black inner feathers and quills get left in the flesh. This is particularly true of the Bronze variety, and, as one body, the buying public are put off by such sights – probably because they are used to seeing the neat, near-shaven finishings of over-ready hens and ducks.

Studying genetics, breeders began experimenting with and breeding white turkeys and while some quill-like inner feathers still remain in the flesh they are barely noticed. The buying public, therefore, find them acceptable.

Around one million turkeys bought at this time of year have been free range. They can be bought online complete with cooking instructions.

From their breeder friends my couple – who are about to spend their last Christmas in England before they resettle in Spain – have learnt that to cover a turkey with foil prevents the skin from crisping. Instead the skin *steams*. And that the recommended cooking time for an average 5kg turkey, at a temperature of 180C or gas mark 4, is two hours, 15 or 20 minutes. After cooking, the bird should rest for 20 minutes to an hour. This period allows the all-important juices to settle.

If ever a bird species has been exploited by us humans it is surely the turkey. Used only to flocking and scratching around in chaff and straw – or sipping from water troughs – their lifespans are short and decided upon once each individual has chipped its way out of an eggshell.

Imprisoned sources of meat I regard turkeys as being. But I savour their portions Christmas cooked, as do thousands of other men and women.

## Burton Point, Wirral Peninsula, Cheshire

My first sighting of the Dee Estuary occurs as, with me in the passenger seat, a friend drives the winding, low-walled and relatively well-wooded roads diverting off the A540, five miles north-west of Chester.

Between the ultra-modern homes and converted farms I see – this Christmas morning – a long finger of smoke-blue water cradled between ranges of low hills on either side; the final aquatic trails of the River Dee, tapering out at some points, closing in at others. As if determined to bring the estuary arm into full focus, the road provides a shelf for the steeply thicketed hillsides to our right. These more relatively modern properties are buttressed; almost a structural part of the land contours which rise to the point of keeping the homes well sheltered from the prevailing wind.

A left turn at Doctor Beeching's long axed railway bridge on the once aptly named Station Road, then, to the right, a somewhat misshapen but partially modernised farmhouse endorses the promise of a family bond because in the porch, and welcoming, stands my eldest son. He is currently serving a contractual term as deputy warden for the Royal Society for the Protection of Birds hereabout.

Once the Christmas pleasantries are exchanged and the ample kitchen-cum-living-room looked over, a turn to face the plate glass windows brings an arm of the estuary within satisfying distance for my ever probing eye. Not that I would want to turn my back upon my son, for he and I have managed somehow to spend every Christmas

Day together since he was born. And if not Christmas Day – perhaps due to marital difficulties on my part – then Boxing Day. He is busy preparing the oven-roast chicken anyway, but my friends and I exchange queries with him regarding the various vistas of land and waterscape down there. And I'm obviously curious to learn something about the hosting districts that have provided him with a relatively spartan income of late.

This four-bedroomed house stands within the renovated outer walls of a farmhouse that served the community possibly back in the seventeenth century. Consequently, there are ghosts. Or at least one. Yet there is not a brooding atmosphere; that eerie feeling of someone looking on. Possibly this is a truly Christmas-loving spirit which, like my son, welcomes visitors.

Between sips of coffee we sit, turning back or sideways to converse while, at the same time, attempting to take in something of the land and water mass at the foot of the sheep-grazed slope.

Today we are looking at a picture postcard arm of the estuary. Pools will, in close-up, be shimmering and rippling due to the increasing force of the wind; stands of reed and marren grass, or its types, will be swaying. But up on the ridge here we see instead pools of fresh or saline water gleaming between the runnels of marshland. Pools which carry the reflective blue of the sky – at least *today.* On black days the pools are black and hardly discernible, due to the icy, wind-driven rain veiling the windows.

On this Christmas morning, however, at Burton Point there is enough sunlit peace to have us believing that there are no such stormy days beyond the windows. But exist they do, my son assures us, while adding that he is more often out in such weather than indoors. Except after dark.

The Dee Estuary. I doubt whether anyone could quote its acreage. Most people describe it as vast or huge as the Rivers Dee and Weaver converge before striking west of the Wirral Peninsula and out across miles of sand, salt and freshwater marsh, while the Mersey floods out on the opposite side of the Wirral and remains hidden from view.

The Romans created a navigation between the Dee mouth and Chester but were not always successful in completing their voyages of trade due to the hidden dangers and often unpredictable turns of the tide. But with the arrival of the Canal Age the necessary Acts of Navigation were granted in 1734, 1744 and 1791.

Below Chester, the boaters of present times are warned of the dangers created by tidal waters and emphasis is upon the experience needed to negotiate these and with craft that are nothing short of seaworthy.

In present times, however, the long arm extending towards the Irish Sea from Burton Point is a nature reserve providing food and habitat for hundreds of birds, plants and crustaceans.

Over the festive meal I recall the location appearing in newspaper cuttings that – perhaps every four or five weeks – were posted through the family home letterbox some two hours drive from here. These postings occurred in the sixties. My eldest son, who has invited my friends and I here today, was with his sister at the toddling stage of their lives. The furniture, rooms, stairs and landing were their equivalent of an adventure park. Downstairs, after work, I read the cuttings which meant nothing to them, even less the Dee Estuary.

Now the situation is reversed. It is I doing the room-to-room explorations and familiarising myself with the furniture, and my son who, carving knife and fork in hand, so enthusiastically describes the situations and adventures he has experienced here.

As for the newspaper cuttings, they were sent to the house by Liverpudlian naturalist, outdoor enthusiast and antiquarian book collector, Reg Lea. We were both members of the then relatively newly-formed British Deer Society, and I had written an article on the herds of red and fallow deer which roamed at will across the parklands close to my home.

As a result of that article Reg, one Saturday morning, took the train from Liverpool to Nottingham and arrived at the deer-park early in the afternoon. We met as strangers, viewing the behaviour patterns of the red deer which were unusually active due to the sexual demand of the autumn rutting season.

Within minutes, and to my surprise, Reg produced a copy of the Society's quarterly bulletin and told me it was an article within it that had motivated him to make the two- or three-hour journey south. And that article, I am delighted to admit, was the one written by me.

But we were, *and are still*, some distance from the Dee Estuary. Over the next few hours Reg and I embarked upon a tour of the deer-park and he mentioned the Liverpool or Cheshire-based naturalist and journalist, Eric Hardy.

Employed as a tutor with the Workers' Education Association, Eric toured many interesting areas within close proximity to the Dee and Mersey estuaries. He also wrote weekly articles for a Liverpool newspaper. Within days of leaving Reg, the first of Eric Hardy's cuttings came to our home courtesy of the Royal Mail, and for years afterwards they continued coming.

Eric Hardy visited the deer-parks as well as the bird and wildfowl reserves. Consequently, I learned such terms as the Ribble Pinkfleet, relating, of course, to the astounding flocks of these northern geese that – in the autumn and winter – assembled there, and the Dee Estuary flocks of greylags – the larger geese – which wintered between the Dee and Mersey estuaries, and probably still do.

Within weeks I was corresponding not only directly with Reg Lea but also Eric Hardy. But at the same time I was happily grounded with my wife, two children and our mortgaged little house taking up the foremost of my thoughts. Trips out to the Dee and Mersey estuaries – along with many contrasting locations – would have to be put aside for future years I decided. And those once 'future years' have at last, and alarmingly, arrived.

This Burton Point house has a small garden surrounded by a low wall. A mature sycamore tempts us out where earlier a robin had displayed its seasonal breast before flickering across the corner to the farm buildings.

On the paved path an elongated fox scat gleams like a green slug. On mentioning this to my son, he tells of an evening or two back when the repeated 'arr' calls of a fox shattered the black silence to the extent of him realising that – in the far-off days when people had to walk by night from the villages and towns all over Britain – certain tracts of land carried the reputation of being haunted when, in fact, it was the rutting calls of dog fox and vixen those people were hearing.

In one corner of the garden the sun strikes warm as I realise that his closest neighbours are *very* close; a young couple, employed as shepherds, and with their mobile home snugly fitted between the farmhouse and the barn and outbuildings inclined bulkily towards the skyline.

While, back indoors, we don thornproofs and walking boots, a male kestrel flies to the low wall and perches with its head sideways as if looking into the room or studying its reflection. A month earlier, we were then told, a stoat literally reared on its hind legs and looked into the room, small predatory eyes gleaming in the winter light, undersides almost starch white and contrasting with the chestnut brown pelage of its body.

Outside there is just space for two cars, a scattering of lane corner sycamores and Rowans, and the smart post and rail fence of a paddock grazing thirty or forty ewes.

At the Station Road corner we turn left, descending with the contour dip, and bringing the bird-frequented marshlands into the afternoon's main excursion. Robins flick individually to perch on marsh-side fence posts, then whirl back to the mossy or ivy-coated walls of the properties or fields to the right.

We are level now with the channels, drains and pools; the former which, at this relatively low water level, appear as no more than singular banked lines dividing the marshes, the latter gleaming like round or elongated mirrors holding the rainbow reflections of an early winter sunset.

The clouds, light and relatively low, are pink or vivid orange, some pale blue edging briefly into grey against a memorable backcloth of turquoise.

The largest of the pools – perhaps twenty acres in extent – burns molten like the glow from a blacksmith's forge. In central position, thirty or forty mallard are settled or feeding, with one drake pintail amongst them. We have no choice but to view them in silhouette, each bird creating a ripple resembling a small pond around the contours of its body.

The cold wind strikes at the cheeks, swiftly moistens the eyes until you realise that you are crying over nothing. And, incredibly, the clouds change colour – more blues coming in now. But not only colour; *the clouds also imperceptibly change shape.*

Ahead to the left the marshscape darkens. A line of cars wedged against the walled fields or properties. 'Scopes are out and the birdwatchers with them.

The westering sun seems to have moved up the estuary somewhat, as if to give us one final encore before nightfall. And, over the smaller gleaming pools, a large tawny grey moth shape hovers.

"Short-eared owl!" my son enthuses.

Today's owl is 50 or 60 feet away, quartering, lifting, rising, then finally settling on a post, the sunlight branding the brown and chestnut tips of its wings as it momentarily holds them outward before swiftly folding them over its back. Statuesque, it perches – this member of a species which habitually uses fence posts on which to perch – and holds the eye of every birdwatcher no matter how many short-eared owls they have 'listed' throughout their respective lifetimes.

The markings of this bird species are so distinctive: black blotches and streaks merging with off-white and the lovely buffish brown of the main body; the eyes, yellow in the western light, emphasise the rounded black of the pupil; the hooked beak is almost hidden by a light frieze of short down.

This particular owl will probably close in on the land and its bankings when it is clear of people, and hover over the thickets listening for the movements of voles or late roosting robins.

More of the owl's winged roundness holds us fast to the binoculars and 'scopes as it lifts silently from the post and describes a spectacular turn that, aided by long silent and distinguishable wing beats, takes it across the marsh and in the direction of the second short-eared owl my son is pointing out. We move on, enthusing at the light, the interchanging rainbow colours of the clouds.

What appears to be a large gull follows the course of a marsh channel. I am about to dismiss it but, binoculars lifted, my friends have stopped. That low flyer is just one of the several white birds in the distance, but appearing as nothing more than pale blobs against the darkening marshlands.

"Little egrets," my son informs us.

When he was bird watching with me and standing the height of my elbow, little egrets were on the rarities list of the birds in Great Britain. Now they are as common as herons in some estuary and coastal districts.

Roosting in groups, little egrets mostly hunt singularly and we watch one stalking – spotless white at distance – along a channel in readiness to snatch a small fish or some similar morsel before making inroads across the marsh where others will gather to roost.

A communicative tap on the shoulder alerts me to my son's sighting of another little egret flying 50 or so feet away, its long legs taut and out beneath its tail. A totally white bird transformed gradually to black by the beams of narrowly thrusting light and increasing shadow, its Chinese print shape further enhanced by the pink and turquoise sky.

A recent count of little egrets hereabout totalled a maximum of 210. And to think that 40 years ago just a single egret would have brought the local birdwatchers here in alarming numbers. Speaking of which, there is a small group of birdwatchers 'glassing the marsh' watching the egrets and short-eared owls.

We approach quietly. My son speaks with them quietly. A sequestered land bordering a tract of bird-frequented marshland is no place to be backslapping, handshaking and conveying seasonal good wishes.

A husband and wife are to the fore. And regulars to the location. Theirs will be one of the cars tucked in by the fence those two or three bends back.

He introduces me. People of around my own age. A man or two in the group walking with a calliper, but woollen hatted and dressed fittingly for this increasing bite of the late afternoon wind.

When the wife of the couple tells me that they have learnt such a lot from my son, and a man offset from the group nods and says, "Yes, he really knows his stuff," an unfamiliar, yet not at all unpleasant, warm swell of pride rises within my chest.

I want then my late wife to be with us and hearing this, and my own father who, on almost every wartime weekend he had free, took me walking into the countryside.

A glance at our respective watches tells that there will be just enough light on the fields' slopes across from Burton Point Farm for watching the barn owl if it chooses to appear. Speaking in low voices, and wishing each other "all the best", we turn to face the eye-watering wind. Across the estuary, here and there along what, at this distance, I take to be the shoreline, are low clusters of yellow light.

"Power stations," my son tells me.

And yet they look so small against the background of hills. Low hills. Undramatic. Beyond them, the *AA Road Atlas of Great Britain* informs me, is the A548 and the Prestatyn to Chester roads leading off. There are also a number of interesting place names: Shotton, Connah's Bay, Flint and Bagillt. But all today are enveloped in the greenish-grey 'smire' of distance.

My son's present home appears misshapen on the skyline now. The marsh is brownish – *mud* brownish – beneath the light, the field slope and drystone walls reminiscent of the Derbyshire Peak District.

The last broad bands of light strike the hill-grazed field to our left. As we approach it, and the cars lined beside the barbed-wire fence, I see a Midlands landscape, a spinney of trees planted like an island in the centre of a cradling green field. *There are so many variations here.*

But, returning to the sheep-grazed field, it is divided by two double ranks of hawthorn hedge that were not planted intentionally as field boundaries. Instead they were planted as windbreaks.

Small flocks of finches and titmice fly in to forage – each for its final meal of the day – and silently quartering the hedgelines at finch-grabbing height is the locally famous barn owl prospecting for its *first meal* of the day, or future night. The owl will also be hunting for small mammals, like shrews, fieldmice and voles. But at this time of the day it has more chance in homing in on the small birds coming in to feed and roost.

When it drops into the tawny-yellow field grasses the owl is lost to view. The tussocks even screen its white front. I believe it is listening, turning its head slowly into the instinctive radar effect that will eventually aid in targeting its first victim of the dusk.

Suddenly the tussocks are forgotten by we onlookers because the owl has risen. It wheels and makes for the fence line, flying along the hedge, turning like a white, slow flapping apparition at the top and then coming down. It quarters the next three lines of hawthorn windbreak in this manner.

Meanwhile, my son locates another hunter. At the top of the field are a line of fence posts. Take the third one in from the left. See? It is higher than the rest, although not according to the landowner's intended design. The fence post is higher because on it a common buzzard is perched.

And facing our direction. It too is seeking a last meal before nightfall. That there is enough prey by way of small mammals and birds here is evident for whatever species about which I am referring; not wasted on energy loss but energy replacement. In other words, if the location lacked the species that serve as prey then it would also lack the species that prey on them. No entity is here or, for that matter, *anywhere*, by pure chance. Each is enmeshed in the vast jigsaw of survival.

The arrival of the buzzard, then, is not coincidental. I believe it saw earlier the barn owl hunting – as apparently it does most afternoons around this time – and homed in to try for prey missed or disturbed by the barn owl.

As we move on up the road, I remark on the continual infusions of winter light out on the estuary arm to our right. There are patches of purple, red and pink centred, with a swathe of sky yellow as an April daffodil. Then from the fields, and high, fly in a skein of greylag geese – the largest of the wild geese and more to type as farmyard geese as any other.

They are too far away for us to pick up their consistent garrulous calls and flightline conversations. Nor are they flying in stiff V formation, as I tend often to imagine them. For instance, there is not one goose to the fore but twenty or thirty all intent on competing for the foremost positions. And, at distance, they appear as an elongated coil of rope, momentarily furling, unfurling and changing shape against the sky. They lower towards their roosting ground, the silvered and metallic black surface of the estuary arm, on which they will remain until daybreak.

Each goose of those many resting, preening and oiling is an individual entity, yet logged and listed by us humans collectively as 'greylag' or a skein of two hundred or three hundred birds.

The light is fading fast now. The sloping field below the farmhouse carries a dark pink mixed with dark green hue. And beyond, in the distance, where the lights of the opposite shoreline appear as no more than yellow pinpoints, the black hand of night is closing in.

Beyond the drystone wall on the field, Dick, the shepherd, kicks a ball for his Border Collie to worry and chase. He comes over, his brim-hatted profile outlined photogenically against the background of pink, green and black.

My son makes the introductions, after which I admit to Dick that I hadn't expected seeing sheep in any great number hereabout. He then tells me that he is responsible for some two thousand put out to the varied grazings on his side of the Wirral peninsula.

His main working quarters – other than the fields – are the outbuildings and barns alongside the farmhouse which my son is currently tenanting. Thus the wind from the west shelters the shepherd's home and quarters from the farmhouse which, in turn, shelters the shepherd's home from the biting rigours of the wind from the east.

Bidding each other farewell we make for the house as Dick and the collie cross the field slopes in front of it.

When the rooms are lit and the central heating turned to an appropriate temperature, this main downstairs room looks somehow bigger than it did when we arrived in sunshine.

The room appeared spacious then but, perhaps because our minds are no longer on the estuary, we tend to discuss the size of this wide windowed room and decide that it is about twenty feet square.

Perhaps once there were two rooms which were eventually knocked into one. There is ample cupboard space and what I take to be a long breakfast bar almost dividing the room. Past residents, therefore, could dine back near the Aga in the colder months and down by the estuary-viewing windows throughout the lighter, warmer days. It is truly an artist's dream residence. Or a writer's retreat. I expect over the years it has been used as both.

Yet, as we sit around the table with plates of sherry trifle before us, there exists – even after dark – the feeling that the place has not been overrun with families and pets. It feels, if anything, relatively new. Untenanted, except by my son.

But the original house was built as a farmer's holding and, in turn, to house other farmers and their families. There would have been many people living here in succession: families; lovers; farmers; shepherds; wildfowlers; and, in more recent times, people with second homes who most probably used this for weekending. The poor lived here originally; the wealthy and middle class in more recent decades. Yet there is little atmosphere in that respect. It feels more as if the house has remained aloof and owned all the people who have lived between its walls, rather than the other way about.

Christmas night television brings people together. We become absorbed by the dancing and celebrity shows. We are stationary. Sheltered. Outside in the blackness all the non-roosting birds are living out small sections of their life cycles. The small mammals, sheep and foxes also.

Around 10.30 one or other of us is nudged by the reminder that we have a two-hour journey ahead. It takes until 11.00 to pack, exchange handshakes and extend final best wishes.

As the car headlights illuminate the low drystone walls and skeletal tree belts, the days of the seemingly far distant summer merge in. For that is when we aim to be visiting again, hopefully for a longer stay. Different territory for us out here.

And so, as instructed, we ignore the sign for Hoylake and turn in the opposite direction for the late Christmas night drive south to the more familiar climes connected by what we hope will be relatively empty motorways.

# BIBLIOGRAPHY

*Know Your Cattle* Jack Byard Old Pond Publishing
*What a Plant Knows* Daniel Chamovitz One World 2013
*What Has Nature Ever Done For Us?* Tony Juniper Profile 2013
*At Home in the Woods* Angrier Down East Books 2015
*The Living Mountain* Nan Shepherd Canongate
*The Worm Forgives the Plough* John Stewart Collis Vintage Collins 1973/2001
*Ice Age Art* Jill Cook British Museum
*Seeds* Thors Hanson Basic Books
*An Eye to the Wind* Peter Scott Eyre and Spottiswood
*Bewick Swan* Eileen Rees T A Poyser
*The Sunlit Summit* Robin Lloyd Jones Sandstone Press

For writing and publishing news, or recommendations of new titles to read, sign up to the Book Guild newsletter: